San Jose: A Personal View

San Jose: A Personal View

Wes Peyton

This limited edition was printed in 1989 as a membership premium by
THE SAN JOSE HISTORICAL MUSEUM ASSOCIATION
635 Phelan Avenue
San Jose, CA 95112

Printed in USA by
The Rosicrucian Press
76 Notre Dame Avenue
San Jose, CA 95113

Editor: Kathleen Muller

Limited first edition, 1989.
Published by the San Jose Historical Museum Association

Library of Congress Cataloging-in-Publication Data

Peyton, Wes, 1925
    San Jose: a personal view / by Wes Peyton.
    109 p. cm.
    Includes index.
    ISBN 0-914139-08-8
    1. San Jose (Calif.) — Social life and customs.   2. San Jose (Calif.) — Biography.   I. Title.
    F869.S394P48   1989
    979.4'74053 — dc20   89-10300
                                                                                       CIP

For Jewel
without whose love and patience
this book
and many other fine and good things
could not have come to pass.

Foreword

The articles contained in this volume, *San Jose: A Personal View,* first appeared in the *San Jose Mercury News* in columns written by Wes Peyton between 1979 and 1983.

The San Jose Historical Museum Association, through its Publication Committee, has chosen to compile a selection of articles from the series that we feel best illustrates San Jose as the city was known by the author and his readers during that period. Some of the articles were written by others, as they made "guest appearances" in Wes's column. We are pleased to include several of these that are especially significant.

The articles have been compiled in sequential order and focus primarily on the individuals and institutions that made their mark after World War II. The value of highlighting their contributions is evidenced by the fact that many of these important people and their significant achievements are unknown to the majority of the area's residents today.

We chose to reprint the articles as they were written originally, without trying to incorporate new information into the text of each article. Instead, whenever possible, the article was updated at its conclusion using uppercase lettering to distinguish it from the original.

Finally, I wish to thank Wes Peyton and the *San Jose Mercury News* for their willingness to allow us to compile these articles into a lasting volume of local history and their generosity in sharing photographs. Thank you also to Virginia Hammerness and Patricia Loomis for their generous assistance in the production of this book.

I hope you enjoy the articles contained in this volume and the accompanying photographs which help to bring each story to life.

Kathleen Muller
Editor

Contents

Foreword i
Contents iii
Introduction 1
The Man Who Led the Fight for the Valley's Water Hole 3
Sharing Thoughts About This Place We Call Home 7
The Garrods Endure, but the County's Farms Are Going 9
Ben Avrech, Keeper of the San Jose Community Conscience 11
Sweeneys Came Here for Education and Ended as Educators 14
High Pay and Sore Hands Working on the Peach Belt 16
Inez Jackson's Tenacious Fight for Equal Rights 19
Geography plus Physics Equals a Perfect Climate 21
Ernie Renzel's Role in the Growth of San Jose 24
San Jose's Biblioteca Is Unique Community Resource 27
From San Jose to America's Servicemen a Gift of the Heart 30
For Years He Wore Two Hats: Union Organizer and Lobbyist 33
'Holy City' Is a Monument to Eccentricity 36
San Jose's First Doctor Caught Gold Fever in Rush of '48 39
Ray Blackmore: Cop and 'Politician' for 42 Years 42
She Didn't Know Anything About Braille, but She Learned 44
Hump Campbell Recalls Days as City Manager 46
Goosetown 49
When Downtown Was Downtown It Had Community Spirit 53
"Making Do" in a Housing Shortage 56
Quest Club Members Get Together to Eat, Drink and Think 58
Bob Doerr Gets People's Attention and Gets Things Done 60
Hayes Mansion Has Historical Past, Condominiums in Its Future 64
Dwight Bissell: A Sense of Humor and a Sense of Health 67

Doctor Worked to Defeat Disease That Almost Defeated Him 70
Clark Bradley's Roots Have Served Him Well 73
John P. McEnery: Old Time Politician...................................... 77
How to Get Your Name on a Journalism Building 80
They Came for the Football Game and Stayed for the War 83
What Really Happened to the Class of '32?................................. 86
Dreaming Along the Banks of the Guadalupe River......................... 89
125 Years' Worth of Celebrating to do at San Jose State's Party 92
Forty Years Later, Japanese-American Internees Fight for Justice 95
Bringing Back the Clang, Clang, Clang of Trolleys and Urchins 99
Foltz for the Defense... 102
Index.. 105

Introduction

This is a little book about (and in some instances by) the men and women who played a part in turning San Jose from a small county seat farm-to-market city into a sprawling metropolis, the capital of what has come to be called Silicon Valley.

The vignettes contained herein are history only in the Churchillian sense (Winie insisted that, properly speaking, there is no history, only biography.) These pieces and others appeared first as a series of occasional columns on the Op Ed pages of the *San Jose Mercury News*. They ran with some regularity from 1979 through 1983, though neither *Mercury News* Editor Rob Elder nor I anticipated the response they would generate among readers of the newspaper. Initially, we envisioned perhaps six or eight articles focusing on some of the movers and shakers who did their moving and shaking in the immediate post-World War II years. Almost as an afterthought we decided to invite *Mercury News* readers to share their recollections of and reactions to San Jose and the Santa Clara Valley. Like Topsy, the column just grew.

Here is how it all began with the first column, dated August 15, 1979:

This is a love story, a sentimental, unabashed, long-playing love story. If it has any relevance or interest beyond the purely personal, it will be because you are part of it.

Forty years ago this November, I fell in love with San Jose.

It was love at first sight.

The ensuing years have altered the shape and size of us both, but the passion endures, at least on my part. I think I know why.

San Jose wears well. That's the overall — and the oversimplified — answer, but it doesn't really satisfy. When a man of 54 still loves that which captured his heart at 14, a great tangle of complexities and subtleties are likely at work. It is also possible the man is a fool. You'll have to be the judge.

All this is by way of introducing a series of columns which will try for a bearing on San Jose and the Santa Clara Valley. I want to explore where we came from and what makes us unique.

1

Wesley G. Peyton, Jr., taken in front of house at 112 Cleaves Avenue, San Jose, May 1940.

No doubt about it, San Jose holds a powerful attraction. No town grows tenfold in 40 years — and keeps on growing —unless it meets some deep-seated need in large numbers of men and women.

Add children to that.

My mother and father arrived in San Jose in November, 1939, with a moon-faced and wide-eyed junior high schooler in tow — me. We came from Fresno, which in 1939 was as close to River City as you were likely to get in California, and that may have had something to do with my immediate enthusiasm for San Jose.

I liked it here right away. Where Fresno was furnace-hot in summer, San Jose was relatively cool. Where Fresno was plate-flat, San Jose was surrounded by hills — and you could see them all day every day back then.

The floor of the Santa Clara Valley was carpeted with fruit trees instead of the grape vines of the San Joaquin. I learned later the trees flowered magnificently in spring. In the winter the grass didn't brown out in San Jose, the way the Bermuda lawns did in Fresno.

But it was the people that sold me on San Jose. Even the girls looked prettier and more sophisticated in San Jose. It didn't take me long to conclude that my parents had transported me to the earthly equivalent of Eden. I knew this was where I wanted to stay.

And stay I did — off and on. In the intervening four decades, I have practiced the journalist's craft on two continents and in some of their principal cities, but I always came home — to San Jose.

Why is that? And why have so many others, including a lot of you, joined me here? It's a question worth examining, because if we can answer it, we will know ourselves better. That's always useful.

Perhaps together we can find some answers that satisfy us. Consider this a standing invitation to write or telephone me here at the *Mercury News.* What do San Jose and Santa Clara County mean to you? We are part of the same community, and I think we may learn a lot if we explore it together.

Perhaps "home" is the operative word in all this. The San Jose area is home. It is where I live. It is where my wife and I have reared two daughters and where we are rearing our son.

Home, according to Robert Frost, is the place where, when you have to go there, they have to take you in. San Jose has always taken me in. I feel it always will.

The Man Who Led the Fight for the Valley's Water Hole

August 22, 1979

Herbert C. Jones died on March 21, 1970, in the fullness of his 89th year. He was a big man, physically and in accomplishment, and it is a commentary on the evanescence of fame that many of the newcomers here probably never heard of him.

We all owe him a lot, and consciously or not we memorialize him every time we sprinkle the lawn, wash the car, drink a glass of water or take a bath.

More than any other single individual, Herb Jones was responsible for bringing water to the Santa Clara Valley — enough water to meet the needs of an urban metropolis. Herb Jones wasn't a hydrologist or an engineer. He was a lawyer and a politician, which fact may serve to put California water matters into perspective.

Water here and across the state has always been as much a political as an engineering problem. It still is: Witness the ongoing tug-of-war over the Federal Bureau of Reclamation's San Felipe Project, which could ultimately bring 145,-000 acre-feet of Sacramento River delta water to Santa Clara and San Benito counties through a tunnel under Pacheco Pass.

Herb Jones backed San Felipe from the beginning. An Iowa-born Quaker, Jones was a fighter when it came to water. Prominently displayed on the back wall of his office was a large, framed print of Frederic Remington's "Fight for the Water Hole." It epitomized Jones' approach to the "water problem" and he put it into words frequently.

"Our problem is not what water will cost," he used to say, "but where we can get it. That community survives which has its own water hole. We are fortunate we have a water hole available — the rivers of the Sierra flowing into the Central Valley."

The last time he said that was in 1962, but Herb Jones and his obsession with the water hole go back to the early decades of this century. It was then that San Jose's — and the Santa Clara Valley's — original water hole was beginning to go dry.

3

Calero Dam, 1938. Photo by Robertson Studios, San Jose. San Jose Historical Museum collections.

By 1905, when Herb Jones, fresh from Stanford Law School, hung out his shingle in downtown San Jose, most people had already forgotten how Fountain Alley got its name. It was named, in fact, for a trench dug to carry away the flow from a runaway artesian well William Campbell sank for the City of San Jose at First and Santa Clara streets.

Artesian gushers were common throughout the valley from the 1850s through the 1880s because of a geological quirk. For millenia, surface water had been seeping into the seemingly bottomless gravel and clay strata that underlie the valley. These aquifers, as they are called, became vast underground reservoirs, and when the first wells were sunk water rushed to the surface under pressure. Thus were born our artesian wells.

However, by 1921 farmers and orchardists had long since reduced the pressure by pumping more water out of the ground than nature was putting back in through natural seepage. The depth-to-water in San Jose wells was dropping; pumping costs were going up; in the north end of the county salt water from San Francisco Bay was beginning to contaminate some wells.

By 1921, Herb Jones had been Santa Clara County's state senator for eight years when he introduced legislation authorizing voters here to form a water conservation district. They managed it in 1929 — on the third election.

There were fights before and after 1929, and Herb Jones was in the thick of them all. The new Santa Clara Valley Water Conservation District hired him as its attorney, and he stayed on for 33 years, retiring in 1962. Mostly the fights were about money, a little less about hydrology and philosophy. Could you "percolate" runoff water into the underground for storage, and if you could, would it cost more than it was worth?

It wasn't until 1934 that district voters approved $2 million in bonds to build the first of the dams and reservoirs that now ring the valley. Two factors finally turned the tide of the struggle for water.

By 1934, the depth-to-water in valley wells had sunk to an all-time low — 140 feet. Also by 1934, the United States, under Franklin D. Roosevelt, was girding to spend itself out of the Great Depression. There was federal money — almost $700,000 of it initially — to help build water conservation works in Santa Clara County.

Within two years, six dams — Almaden, Calero, Coyote, Guadalupe, Stevens Creek and Vasona — were built, and together they stored almost 44,000 acre-feet of runoff. That is, in a wet year they did.

Mostly the years were wet enough, and from 1936 through World War II, winter rains captured in the six reservoirs were released gradually during spring and summer months to trickle through the gravelly stream beds and downstream percolation ponds into the underground aquifers. The water table began to rise again.

These were the years when it became evident to Herb Jones and others that post-war growth would almost surely threaten the water hole again. They got ready to import water from northern California's rivers and streams. Again there were fights, and again they hinged on money.

Herbert C. Jones, (center) talks over old times with State Senator Jack Thompson and Joe Beck, secretary of the Senate. Mercury News photo.

Could valley residents afford to bring "state," much less "federal," water here?

Herb Jones' answer was always the same: Could we afford *not* to pay the price?

Against this backdrop, the Santa Clara Valley Water Conservation District built two more major facilities, the giant Anderson dam and reservoir that impounds 91,280 acre-feet of Coyote River water in the foothills of the Diablo range, and Lexington dam and reservoir, on Los Gatos Creek south of Los Gatos. Lexington, completed in 1952, impounds 20,210 acre-feet and brings the district's storage capacity to 153,437 acre-feet.

In practical terms, Lexington marked the end of "local" water development. There are no new sources to tap — here.

But the effort didn't stop there, and it hasn't stopped yet. In 1965, the district began to receive the first water from the Sacramento River delta. It was delivered through the state's South Bay Aqueduct, and at first all if it went underground. By 1969, land subsidence was largely under control in the San Jose area.

Subsidence occurs when too much water is pumped out of the clay and gravel aquifers; they simply collapse and they can't be expanded again. As an aquifer is squeezed, it loses the ability to store water in its compressed portion. The loss is permanent.

By way of illustration, the Santa Clara County Courthouse, on North First Street in San Jose, began to sink in 1919. It dropped 13 feet before it stopped sinking in 1969. Groundwater recharge, in good part from the South Bay Aqueduct, is responsible for the holding action.

In 1951-52, the Santa Clara County Flood Control and Water Conservation District was formed, with the County Board of Supervisors in charge. Its main function was flood control, though there was some over-lapping with the long-established Water Conservation District. Sensibly, the two merged in 1974 to become the present County Water District.

And Herb Jones was in the thick of the fight — for merger and for San Felipe water — until he retired in 1962. He had spent 33 years with the

Water Conservation District and another eight years before that getting it started.

Quaker though he was, Herb Jones knew the importance of a water hole in the arid West, and he spent a lifetime fighting for ours.

So here's a toast — in good, fresh water — to the memory of Herbert C. Jones.

Vasona Dam on the Los Gatos Creek. San Jose Chamber of Commerce photo. San Jose Historical Museum collections.

Sharing Thoughts About This Place
We Call Home

August 29, 1979

Beauty is the key word, I think.

San Jose and the Santa Clara Valley are beautiful, which explains why they're easy to love and hard to leave.

At least, that's what I think a lot of you have been telling me in telephone calls, brief notes and longer letters over these past three weeks.

And if I read you rightly, the beauty we experience here is more than visual. We can feel it in the gentle climate, smell it in our gardens, taste it in the fruit and vegetables we still grow and the wine we press here. A lot of you see beauty in the way we try to make each other feel at home, and I think you've got something there.

I asked you to share your thoughts, feelings and recollections about this place we call home, and you've come through grandly. Here (along with my grateful thanks) is some of what you've been telling me.

From Karen Attaway, who came here in the summer of 1960 from lush, green — and mountainous — Tacoma, Washington:

"How can I survive in this alien place? thought I. 'Everything looks burned up,' said mother when she came to visit. But my husband was new, the mortgage was new and the days went by.

"Then, imperceptibly at first, I began to fall in love.

"Perhaps it began when I noticed that the summer hills were not brown at all! They are gold as anyone can see. And when the breezes blow, the gold becomes ripples, as waves in a sea. And barren? Surely not, but proud! Boastful of every graceful curve and roll . . .

"Today my fondness is full-blown. Sun-spoiled and free, I know I will not stray. This is my home . . .

Angela M. Weber, late of Honolulu, put it this way: ". . . The weather is almost perfect. As one whose body works like a solar heater, I am at home here . . . I have seen the best fruits and vegetables in San Jose, better produce than anywhere I've ever lived (six different states). And the best prices, too. In most cases, they're free, as our neighbors are very generous.

"You have friendly people. Most of these are transplants, like myself, so maybe we have an immediate common bond . . .

"But when it comes right down to it, San Jose took us in when we needed a home. We're here and we'll probably stay."

Norma Slavit, a native San Franciscan, came down the Peninsula — for good — 17 years ago. Fine schools and reasonably priced housing were prime factors in the Slavit family decision, she says, adding:

"As our population increases, I hope we never outgrow, or lose sight of, the wonderful quality so many residents hold dear — the dignity and importance of human rights."

Donna McBeth and her family arrived from Dallas, Texas, about the same time the Slavit's came down from San Francisco. The McBeths settled in Santa Clara and found "the schools, community activities and cultural opportunities . . . above average." Mrs. McBeth links past and future:

"Our history is short, compared to European countries, but we are beginning to appreciate our architectural and artistic beginnings and to preserve them. From a "throw-away society" we are learning to become appreciative of our resources so that whatever it was that attracted us and keeps us here will not be lost forever to others . . ."

Emil Kissel of Saratoga finds this area's most attractive feature to be "the climate for all kinds of creative enterprise . . . The challenge is to solve our environmental and human problems; I can see the world's future (being) developed here . . ."

The Garrods Endure, but the County's Farms Are Going

September 5, 1979

Dick Garrod stirred the swizzle stick in his brandy-and-soda, knitted up his bushy eyebrows and broke into a characteristically wry grin:

"It's high desert up there. I love it, but it's still high desert. The growing season's short, and it's all field crops — but if you want to farm, and to leave something for the next generation, you have to go where there's still land at a reasonable price."

Richard S. Garrod knows about land and about farming — and about the generations.

His grandfather and grandmother, David and Sophia Garrod, were school teachers who emigrated from England to the Santa Clara Valley in 1892 for their health. They bought 15 acres of flatland near Cambrian school and a year later traded it for 110 acres high up on Monte Bello Ridge overlooking what is now Stevens Creek Park. In 1893 nobody thought the hillsides could be farmed.

David Garrod thought otherwise. He and Dick's father, R. V. "Vince" Garrod, planted the hillsides — a little at a time — in prunes, apricots, some walnuts and wine grapes.

In time the 110 acres grew to almost 250, and the Garrods of Saratoga became synonymous with agriculture in Santa Clara County. Almost a century later, the Garrods endure, but the chances are farming won't — not here, anyway.

That's what Dick was talking about the other night.

He, his older brother, Vincent S. Garrod, and his sister, Louise Cooper, still live on Monte Bello Ridge with their families, and they're still farmers. But the Garrods farm as a trust now and their largest holdings are almost 300 miles to the northeast, on the "high-desert" that Dick loves. They have 1,500 acres in cereal grains, alfalfa and sugar beets at the south end of Honey Lake, on the east side of the Sierra Nevada mountains in Lassen County.

"We've only got an acre of prunes left at the home ranch," Dick mused, "for old times' sake, I guess. The farms are going."

Twenty years ago, more than 71,000 acres of prunes, apricots, walnuts and their cousins still

9

flourished in Santa Clara County. Last year the County Agricultural Commissioner's office could count barely 13,000 acres of them. Sooner or later, farmers who want to farm will be forced to do it somewhere else. For the Garrods of Saratoga, that time has come sooner rather than later.

The gnarled oaks, the rolling grasses, perhaps a dozen acres of wine grapes, another 15 acres of Christmas trees — and the limestone outcroppings of Monte Bello Ridge — still make up the Garrod Farm, but its the Garrod Farm Stables now. It caters to the occasional rider and to those who want to board their own horses, and it serves between 60,000 and 70,000 persons a year. The stables, like other Garrod family farming enterprises, are actively managed by Dick's brother, Vince.

Dick and Vince are, in a way, component parts of their father, R. V. Garrod. By the time he died at age 92 — seven years ago in his bed on the home ranch and not in some sterile institution — Vince Garrod had proved two points little understood by urbanites. The first is that economically, farmers no less than revolutionaries must hang together if they would avoid hanging separately. The second is that farmers lose when farming and politics part company.

Vince the elder was both farmer and politician. Vince the younger is the quintessential farmer; Dick, his younger brother, is the farmer-lobbyist-politician.

In 1909 Vince Garrod the elder organized the California chapter of the Farmers Educational and Cooperative Union. Its message to farmers: Organize grower cooperatives or remain at the mercy of the large canners and food processors. Vince's neighbors got the message and in 1928 formed the California Prune and Apricot Growers Association, now known as Sunsweet Growers. It's still going strong.

Vince knew farmers needed insurance as much as any businessman, and he helped build what is today's Farmers Insurance Group.

Finally, Vince knew the successful farmer must tend his legislature as carefully as his fields and orchards. He lobbied Sacramento for laws that would help farmers directly — laws affecting

R. V. "Vince" Garrod, from *The Sunsweet Story* by Robert Couchman. San Jose Historical Museum collections.

water development, soil conservation, marketing procedures and taxes, for example. Nor did Vince overlook government's ability to assist the farmer indirectly.

The University of California owes its School of Veterinary Medicine at Davis to R. V. Garrod. In 1941 he persuaded the Legislature to authorize the school and appropriate $500,000 for its establishment. A world war intervened, and the first 42 students didn't arrive at Davis until 1948. The school now graduates 128 doctors of veterinary medicine every year, and the campus' main street is named Garrod Boulevard.

By the time he died, everybody around here called him "Mr. Agriculture." He liked that. He'd earned it.

THE GARROD FAMILY STILL OPERATES THE RIDING STABLE ON MONTE BELLO RIDGE, BUT DICK GARROD, WHO SUPPLIED MUCH OF THE BIOGRAPHICAL INFORMATION ABOUT HIS FATHER, DIED IN FEBRUARY, 1988.

Ben Avrech, Keeper of the San Jose Community Conscience

September 12, 1979

There he was, spread across a two-page layout in the April 11, 1961, issue of *Look* magazine: Ben Avrech — Eastside merchant, civic leader, human rights activist — perched atop a San Jose Fire Department aerial ladder. He was smiling patiently into the camera while, behind him, a subdivision of newly minted single-family homes sprawled away to infinity.

It was a fascinating tableau at the time; in the perspective of 18 years, it is even more so.

Look had just named San Jose an All American City, partly because of its phenomenal growth and partly because San Jose was taking steps to be forehanded about racial and ethnic tensions. Industrialization and urbanization had turned melting pots into pressure cookers back East —and would do so again close to home in the '60s. Remember Watts?

That's what Ben was doing up on the ladder truck, smiling at the *Look* photographer. He knew it could happen here; he was betting it wouldn't. It didn't, thanks to Ben Avrech and a great many like-minded men and women. We all know that today; it's history. Back in 1961 it was a gamble.

Ben Avrech would scoff at the notion that he is, or was, a keeper of the community conscience, but in 1961, when San Jose was tagged an All American City, Ben was already into his third year as chairman of the San Jose Human Relations Commission. Such agencies are commonplace today; in Santa Clara County, circa 1961, the San Jose commission was a pioneering effort.

And it was Ben's baby. In 1957 he prodded the City Council to study whether San Jose even needed such a body. He bird-dogged the study and lobbied the council to accept its recommendation. When the council created the commission in 1958, it named Avrech chairman. His fellow commissioners continued him in the job for four more years. That helps explain why he was up on the ladder truck.

Look magazine chose, appropriately, to cast Ben as a symbol: He was Mr. San Jose. He was one of the forces that made this town special, made it different from other cities on their way to the municipal big time.

11

ALL AMERICA CITIES

From *Look* magazine, April 11, 1961, Bob Vose, photographer. Ben Avrech, Chairman of San Jose's Human Relations Council and Commission high above the City of San Jose. Photo courtesy of Ben Avrech.

How Ben Avrech arrived at the top of that aerial ladder is part of San Jose's history, too, but it isn't as well known as it should be. For those who would know San Jose better, that's too bad. Here, then, is some neglected personal history:

Ben Avrech was born in 1906 in eastern Europe. Had he stayed there, he would have been, variously, a Romanian, a Russian or a Czech. His birthplace changed hands frequently, which was unsettling for everybody and deadly dangerous for Jews, especially for educated, relatively prosperous Jews.

Ben's father, Henry, was a miller and grain exporter; he was also one of the few well-educated men in his small community, and he saw privilege as responsibility. He wrote letters, managed accounts and served as unofficial counselor for the less literate. It was this sense of civic responsibility that — ultimately — sent the Avrech family packing.

The 1917 Bolshevik revolution plunged Russia into a bloody civil war. For years, the Red Army battled Czarist "White Russian" forces. Both sides distrusted and systematically harrassed Jews such as Henry Avrech. To the Reds, he was a capitalist; after all, didn't he deal in exports? To the White Russians he was a communist; after all, didn't he write letters for (and probably organize) the peasants?

By 1921 Henry Avrech had had enough. He was tired of hiding periodically from Russians, Red and White. He fled with his wife, Anna, and their six children — four boys and two girls. Ben was 15 at the time.

The family made its way west, helped by other Jews and Jewish organizations. That was tradition, of course. Two thousand years of exploitation, persecution and dispossession have taught Jews a cardinal truth: Survival depends on cooperation.

Ben Avrech internalized the lesson on his way to San Jose via Antwerp, Montreal and New York. In the course of climbing the economic ladder from a $6-a-week laborer in a Montreal shoe factory to owner of the Mayfair department store at 21st and Santa Clara streets, he expanded

12

Ben Avrech, 1969. Mercury News photo.

on it. Cooperation among all colors, races and creeds isn't just a noble idea; it's everybody's survival mechanism.

It's also what gives validity to any human rights movement, and so it was natural, probably inevitable, that Ben Avrech should gravitate first to the Anti-Defamation League of B'nai B'rith, which is dedicated to combatting anti-Semitism, and through the ADL to the Santa Clara Valley Council for Civic Unity. The civic unity group, with Ben as spokesman, kept pressure on the San Jose City Council to form a Human Relations Commission.

It seems so long ago now. The city commission, formed in 1958, acquired its first paid staff member in 1963. It was another 10 years before Santa Clara County formed its own Human Relations Commission. City and county organizations merged into a single, countywide unit in 1976.

The fight against discrimination goes on — and so does Ben Avrech. He sold the Mayfair department store in 1971 and "retired." But he can't break the habits of a lifetime. Today, among other activities, he's helping resettle Russian refugee families here. Survival depends on cooperation.

IN RETIREMENT, BEN AVRECH STILL LIVES IN HIS HOME IN SAN JOSE.

Sweeneys Came Here for Education and Ended as Educators

September 26, 1979

Over the years, settlers have become San Joseans for a lot of reasons: The land was fertile, the climate suited their health, jobs were plentiful, friends or relatives came ahead and beckoned.

Charles and Ida Sweeney moved here from Nevada City because San Jose was the best place for their daughter, Mardell, to become a school teacher. The year was 1922, and Mardell was 18.

In 1922 the streetcar tracks ended at Delmas and Willow streets. Willow Glen was a separate, incorporated city and Cupertino was a country crossroad. Los Gatos was *way* out, the jumping off point for Santa Cruz.

In 1922, San Jose had a population of 43,000 and San Jose State Teachers College already enjoyed a reputation as the best education school on the West Coast. Everybody in the Mother Lode country who cared about such things knew of the teachers' college down in San Jose.

One of those who knew was Ida Sweeney. She wanted Mardell to have the best, and so did Mardell's father, Charles, a painter and paperhanger.

But they didn't send Mardell off to college. Not the Sweeneys. Ida packed up the whole family and moved to San Jose. As soon as he could, Charles sold his Nevada City business and joined them. He went to work for a painting contractor here for $9 a day.

If you get the impression from all this that education means a great deal to the Sweeneys, you'd be right. And education in this city and state has been shaped considerably because of that passion.

Before we go further, I'll confess that this isn't really Mardell Sweeney's story. Oh, she graduated from San Jose State and taught for a few years, but ultimately she became secretary to the State Superintendent of Public Instruction and, later, secretary to the State Board of Architectural Examiners.

This is really the story of Mardell's kid brothers, Bill and Ben.

William G. was 14, Ben only six, when the Sweeneys moved into the big, old-fashioned house on Seventh Street across from San Jose

State and down the block from San Jose High School.

In those days, San Jose High was nestled on a corner of the college campus, on the spot where the San Jose State University administration building now stands. Neither boy got very far from there geographically; professionally, it's another story.

Bill Sweeney was graduated from San Jose State in 1930 and went off to teach English in Centerville (now part of the City of Fremont). Later he moved to Menlo Park and taught in the Menlo School and College while working for his master's degree at Stanford.

In 1934, Menlo discovered the Depression and cut Bill's $2,200 annual salary in half. Sweeney went job hunting and was offered a one-year, $1,800, speech instructor's post at San Jose State. Bill took the job and stayed on for 37 years.

Dr. William G. Sweeney, 1967 Mercury News photo.

When he retired in 1971, Dr. William G. Sweeney had headed the SJSU School of Education for 20 years. He was also making more money; full professors by then earned $23,000 a year.

He had seen the faculty grow from eight (six women and two men, himself included) to 80. The entire college had an enrollment of 1,700 in 1934. This fall, SJSU enrolled 26,951 students, nearly 2,000 of them in the School of Education.

Bill Sweeney declines to estimate the number of school teachers he has loosed on almost two generations of California youngsters, but surely they must be counted in the thousands. At one point, in the post-World War II boom years, San Jose State annually graduated more elementary teachers than any other school in the country; only Michigan State produced more high school teachers.

And Brother Ben? Yes, he went into education, too. He taught in San Jose for 35 years, serving as principal of San Jose and Pioneer High Schools before moving on to San Jose Community College District. He was dean of continuing education at City College for 14 years, retiring in 1976.

Carrying the family tradition further, two of Ben's sons are teachers; Bill's son, Donald, is principal of Santa Clara County Science School in Boulder Creek.

What happened to Charles and Ida? you ask. Their roots were three generations deep in the Mother Lode, and they moved back to Nevada City after the kids finished school. It seemed a fair enough bargain. San Jose educated their three children, and two of them stayed here to repay that debt in kind and in full.

BILL SWEENEY LIVES IN RETIREMENT IN SAN JOSE. HIS BROTHER, BEN, IS ALSO RETIRED AND LIVING IN CAMPBELL.

High Pay and Sore Hands Working on the Peach Belt

October 3, 1979

SAN JOSEANS HAVE BEEN DRYING PRUNES AND APRICOTS AND CANNING ASSORTED FRUITS AND VEGETABLES FOR LONGER THAN THE OLDEST OLD-TIMER CAN REMEMBER. IN THE THIRD AND FOURTH DECADES OF THIS CENTURY, FOOD PROCESSING DOMINATED THE AREA'S ECONOMY.

WHEN FEWER THAN 70,000 PERSONS CALLED SAN JOSE HOME, BETWEEN 20,000 AND 25,000 MEN, WOMEN AND CHILDREN TROOPED INTO MORE THAN TWO DOZEN CANNERIES HERE EACH SUMMER. THEY SWEATED THERE TO HELP PUT THEMSELVES THROUGH SCHOOL OR TO AUGMENT THE FAMILY INCOME. IT WAS HARD, HOT, SMELLY WORK, BUT IT PAID WELL AND IT WAS BIG BUSINESS. THE PAYROLL APPROACHED 18 MILLION PRE-INFLATION DOLLARS.

TODAY A HALF-DOZEN CANNERIES THROUGHOUT SANTA CLARA COUNTY ARE ALL THAT REMAIN OF THIS ONCE PRE-EMINENT INDUSTRY. THE SIX TOGETHER EMPLOY FEWER THAN 4,000 PERSONS AT SEASON'S PEAK. THE CANNERY IN WHICH JEWEL PEYTON WORKED AS A GIRL IS NO LONGER WITH US UNDER ANY NAME.

ONE WHO CARRIES THE MEMORIES OF CANNERY WORK WITH HER TO THIS DAY IS MY WIFE. LET HER TELL YOU ABOUT IT:

BY JEWEL PEYTON

I spent the summer of my 16th year working on the peach belt in one of San Jose's premier canneries, then called Barron Gray Packing Co. It's now Dole-Hawaiian.

This is no how-hard-life-was-when-I-was-young story. I was only one of thousands of young people whose labor was desperately needed to harvest and pack the tons of fruit produced in Santa Clara Valley during the man-power-short years of World War II.

The fruit growers and canners were scraping the bottom of the barrel, and there we were, joined by an army of housewives eager to pick up extra money during the summer.

We were well received. My take-home pay, after deductions, was $72 a week. From what I remember of prices at the time, I estimate it would take four or five times that amount today to equal the purchasing power of those 1945 dollars.

It wasn't easy come, easy go. For one thing, it didn't come all that easy, and for another, when you work an emergency war schedule of 10¼ hours a day, six days a week, there isn't much time for shopping.

Those hours, incidentally, were only for women and girls. Boys and men were allowed to work seven days a week.

Each morning, clad in the classic pedal pushers and bobby sox of the day, I rode my bike from our home at South Twelfth and San Fernando streets to Barron Gray, at the corner of Fifth and Martha streets. There I had a few minutes for chatter with arriving schoolmates, all similarly clothed and all carrying the cannery worker's uniform—a white hat peaked like a nurse's cap in front with a net body to confine stray hairs, a plastic apron, and rubber gloves.

I donned my cap and apron and went to my appointed place on the peach belt, where, before the machines started, I carefully dusted the insides of my gloves with talcum powder before putting them on.

The peaches that passed before us on the belt were on their way to be diced for fruit cocktail, and the sole purpose of the peach belt was to prevent ruin to the expensive knives in the dicing machines. The knives could be ruined by only one thing—a peach pit. We had to make sure that no peach pit ever reached the dicing machines.

I cannot imagine a more boring job, or one more debasing to the body, the mind and the spirit. We stood on wooden pallets placed over a cement floor. Because fruit was dropped often, the floor was hosed periodically as we worked, treating our entire bodies, and especially our feet, to a several-times-daily steam bath. There was no air conditioning and not enough ventilation.

The peaches had been scalded, dipped in a

Workers at the Del Monte cannery, San Jose, 1943. Gabriel Moulin Studios, San Francisco. San Jose Historical Museum collections.

caustic solution to remove the skins, cut in half, and, usually, pitted. A large overhead machine shook these peach halves onto the belt. We had to watch the belt carefully, remove the few peaches with pits or fragments of pits and throw them into a tub beside us.

The halves that landed cut side down had to be turned over to see if they held pits. There were many such halves, and our basic motion was turning over peaches and throwing the occasional one with a pit into a tub.

It was hot, steamy, smelly work, fatiguing to the legs, back, neck and arms. Inevitably, the mixture of warm peach juice and the peel removing solution, which the workers said was lye, trickled down inside our gloves, causing painful rashes of the hands.

But, worst of all, the job provided us with nothing to think about. At first I was happy with this, rejoicing in enough time, at last, to daydream to my heart's content. Then I discovered an amazing truth: Even a highly romantic, imaginative teen-aged girl cannot daydream 61½ hours a week. I ran out of material after two days.

Spending an extended period in an environment which provided no mental stimulation whatsoever was painful. After an initial bout of self-pity, I began to realize there are people who put up with equally boring tasks all their lives. I decided, still being a romantic, that people who find fun in their work should not be paid nearly so highly as those who are bored at work. I had yet to learn that psychic gratification, however vital it may be, doesn't pay the bills.

I finally left the peach belt about one week short of the season's end with a severe rash that was peeling the skin off my hands. I came away with a new confidence in the limits of my endurance, a lot of money, and undying respect for all those who perform menial tasks.

But to this day, I can't eat canned peaches.

Inez Jackson's Tenacious Fight for Equal Rights

October 10, 1979

If you had to characterize Inez C. Jackson in a single word, you could do a lot worse than "tenacious."

At age 72, Inez Jackson has not only survived, she has prevailed against odds that would have wilted the less determined.

But, then, you don't grow up black in a white society and manage to turn that society around, even just a little, by being timid.

You don't today, and you surely didn't when Inez Jackson was rearing her family and forcing San Joseans, gently but firmly, to face their largely unadmitted racial prejudices. That took courage, tact, warmth, humor, compassion and intelligence, all of which Inez Jackson possesses in ample measure.

It also took tenacity. It was no quick and easy job. For that matter, it's a job that isn't finished yet; some say it will never be finished. Inez Jackson isn't one of them. She's bullish on human beings of all colors and persuasions although she has few illusions about any of them.

That's what makes her, and her contribution to San Jose, so special.

If Leon Jackson hadn't come West in 1942 to help win World War II by building ships in Richmond, wife Inez and the six Jackson children may never have become part of San Jose. That would have been a real loss because Inez Jackson's gift is that she made us *see* her, literally see her and other black San Joseans.

Not that they hadn't been here for some time: the first AME Zion church, which stood for years at the corner of Fourth and San Antonio streets, was incorporated in 1883. The land for it was donated to the church 20 years earlier than that. San Jose's black community goes back a long way, but before Inez Jackson it was largely invisible.

"One of the first things I noticed here," she recalled the other day, "was that you never saw a black person in any public capacity. No black waiters, or clerks, or bank tellers — or teachers. You'd go in the schools, and there were no pictures of black Americans on the walls. I didn't think that was right."

Inez Jackson. Mercury News photo.

San Jose had no legal segregation, but it discriminated against blacks in its own, more subtle way. It pretended they didn't exist; those few inconsiderate enough to disprove that by living here were told the really good jobs weren't for them; they weren't qualified. That went for the good housing, too.

Inez Jackson holds a degree in mathematics from Langston University, in Langston, Oklahoma, and she was teaching school in Shawnee, Oklahoma when Leon sent for her and the children in 1944. They settled in San Jose, buying a small house in the *sal si puedes* ("get out if you can") barrio of East San Jose, because nobody was selling homes to blacks in Oakland in those days. Leon could commute to the shipyard, but Inez couldn't teach. San Jose wasn't hiring black teachers in 1944.

Inez picked prunes and worked in the canneries for a couple of years ("they told me nobody would hire a black for anything else") before taking Harry Truman at his word. The president said the Post Office should be color-blind. Inez took the civil service examination and

became the first black postal clerk in San Jose's history. She worked there 24 years before retiring.

That isn't all she did. She determined to become visible. She was a constant visitor at her children's schools, keeping a professional eye on their teachers. She joined the Parent-Teacher Association, the National Association for the Advancement of Colored People, the Antioch Baptist Church and the Garden City Women's Club.

She became a familiar sight at city council and county supervisors' meetings. She let government know that she and other black San Joseans existed and that they intended to be treated as equals; it was their right. She passed the same word to every private body that would listen. It took a long time, but it worked.

Inez Jackson became a member of the first San Jose Human Relations Commission and the first black president of the San Jose Young Women's Christian Association. She helped persuade the Elks Club to give up its fund-raising blackface minstrel shows in the Civic Auditorium, and she saw her oldest daughter, Agnes, become a public school teacher (but not here — Agnes is now a counselor at Sacramento High School).

"I came to like San Jose," she mused recently, "even though I was afraid at first. There are good people here; there were from the first, but they had to be helped to see."

Inez Jackson helped. In fact, she's still helping. Inflation, economic uncertainty and Proposition 13 have combined to threaten some of the economic and social gains blacks and other minority groups worked hard to win in the 1960s, she says, and that's reason enough to keep busy.

She's right; she's also tenacious.

AT 82, INEZ JACKSON HAS SLOWED DOWN A BIT — BUT JUST A BIT. SHE STILL ATTENDS SOME OF THE MEETINGS OF THE GARDEN CITY WOMEN'S CLUB AND THE NAACP, BUT SHE SPENDS MOST OF HER TIME NOW WITH HER FAMILY, WHICH HAS GROWN TO INCLUDE 13 GRANDCHILDREN AND 16 GREAT-GRANDCHILDREN.

Geography plus Physics Equals a Perfect Climate

November 7, 1979

I don't know if the best things in life really are free, but I do know that one of the best things about life in these parts is free — and taken so for granted that we rarely think about it consciously.

I'm talking about the climate.

It's always great, or at least predictable, and it never stays disagreeable for long, so what's to think about? Who thinks about his shoes if they don't pinch?

A lot of you, though, have been forcing me to think about what I've been taking for granted. You haven't been here long enough to become blase about the weather, and you talk about it at length in your letters. Typical is the comment of Jean L. Wunder, a native of Sussex, England. She's been a San Josean for nine years now, and she concluded a recent letter thusly:

"We love the hills and enjoy the differences in color they bring us at different times of the year . . . the glorious sunsets we experience, the good way of life it has given us . . . *the best climate ever . . .*"

The best climate ever. It is that, but what makes it the best?

For answers, I spent a morning recently with Dr. Christopher A. Riegel, chairman of the department of meteorology at San Jose State University. He was cheerful and patient, and he helped me understand the weather a little better. Let me pass on Dr. Riegel's explanation in simplified, but I hope serviceable, form.

The Santa Clara Valley enjoys a fabulous climate because it's in the right place at the right time. We're comfortably installed in the north temperate zone, which gives us a head start on good weather. Still, if our geography were different, we would have different weather.

Our valley is wedged between the Diablo range on the east and a penny-ante ridge of forested hills on the west known locally as the Santa Cruz Mountains. (Actually, they're a northern spur of the Santa Lucia range.) Just over those western hills lies the Pacific Ocean, the flywheel of our weather engine.

The earth's surface is 72 percent water, and the Pacific Ocean, the world's biggest puddle,

Looking northeast from ridge above Graystone Lane, San Jose, 1955. Photograph by Robert B. Mercure, San Jose. San Jose Historical Museum collections.

churns out our weather in conjunction with the sun, the rotation of the earth and — most critical — the air.

For most of the year, a huge mountain of air, known to meteorologists as the subtropical Pacific high pressure system, controls our weather. The Pacific high extends all the way to Japan, and it tends to follow the sun. It slips southward in winter, letting the upper atmosphere's eastward-rushing jet stream slam us with those warm, wet storms that breed in the Pacific's tropical latitudes. Now and then a stray norther will blast out of the Gulf of Alaska and dust us with snow, but that's only now and then. For the most part, the Pacific keeps us wet and relatively warm in the winter.

Putting winter storms aside, here's how the Pacific high interacts with our geography to keep us cool in the spring and summer. The process starts to the east of the Diablo range, in the Sacramento and San Joaquin valleys. As a generality, you can say it's cool here because it's hot there.

As the sun beats down, the interior valleys get hot. Then the air over the valleys gets hot. As the air heats up, it expands and its pressure drops. In time, the air pressure over the Sacramento-San Joaquin becomes lower than the pressure of our old friend, the Pacific high.

Just as water flows downhill, air flows from areas of high pressure to areas of low pressure. When the air pressure over the interior valleys

22

is lower than the air pressure over the Pacific, marine air begins to flow shoreward. It passes over thousands of miles of cold water, getting colder by the mile.

By the time this marine air pours through the Golden Gate and the coastal mountain passes closer to us — the San Bruno and Crystal Springs gaps — it's cold enough to provide us with natural air conditioning.

This ebb and flow of air tends to follow a five-to-seven-day cycle as pressures build up and are neutralized over and over again. Air is never still for long because its temperature is always fluctuating. That's why our occasional hot spells never last too long.

So you see, our mild climate is the result of a combination of geography and physics. If it weren't for those coastal hills holding off the marine air while the valleys heat up, we'd probably be nothing but a chilly, windswept littoral. We got those mountains way back in geologic time, and they're still working for us.

All things considered, who can say we haven't been greatly blessed, even unto the present?

Ernie Renzel's Role in the Growth of San Jose

December 5, 1979

The voice on the telephone crackled with barely suppressed mischief: "Ca va, mon vieux? Tu es bien ecupe?"

It was Ernie Renzel. The French repartee is a running joke between us and has been for nearly 30 years. It dates from my days as City Hall reporter, or more accurately from when I quit being City Hall reporter to study in Paris.

In the late 1940s Ernie was mayor of San Jose. Actually, he was president of the city council; we didn't have a mayor then, but everybody called Ernie mayor anyway. He was (and is) the sort who lends stature to whatever enterprise engages him; that includes travel and foreign languages, a couple of his hobbies.

Ernie was never persuaded I would master French, and he's been checking periodically since I got back. He called the other day to suggest a column on Frazier O. Reed, a real estate magnate and bank director who died in 1969. Reed's grandfather, James Frazier Reed, came to California in 1846 with the ill-fated Donner Party

and ultimately settled in San Jose, where Frazier O. was born in 1882.

In his day Frazier Reed wheeled and dealed with the best, entitling him to more than a footnote in city history. But for my money, Ernie Renzel's story has more to tell us about how we managed the transition from small city to metropolis.

Ernest H. Renzel Jr., 72, is a second-generation San Josean (his father was born about where the lobby of the now-shuttered Fox Theater stands on South First Street). His grandfather, a baker, emigrated from Germany and settled here in the 1850s.

Ernie grew up in the old Fourth Ward, south and a bit west of today's downtown, and he remembers when a soap factory flourished on the banks of the Guadalupe River and when the electric tower at Santa Clara and Market streets collapsed. Educated in San Jose schools and at Stanford University, he entered the family's wholesale grocery business.

He was running it by the time World War II began to work its profound changes on San Jose.

He and some others styling themselves the San Jose Progress Committee set out to direct that change. They succeeded beyond their dreams.

In 1944, a series of unrelated and wholly coincidental events caused six of the seven seats on the San Jose City Council to fall vacant. It seemed to Ernie and a clutch of businessmen and labor leaders a good time to challenge the power of the era's reigning political boss, a liquor distributor and ambulance operator named Charlie Bigley.

Ernie Renzel, Jr., 1968. Mercury News photo.

"It was penny-ante, really," Ernie mused the other day. "They could have stolen the city blind if they'd wanted to, but they didn't. Charlie just wanted to see that his friends got jobs and promotions with the city — you know, on the police and fire departments and like that. He did it the traditional way, through political contributions to the City Council. Charlie always had a majority of the Council, which kept the city manager (then Clarence B. Goodwin) in office. The manager hired the police and fire chief. It was all very neat."

But it fell apart when Ernie and the Progress Committee decided to run a slate of candidates, six men for six seats. On May 1, 1944, Ernie was elected to the San Jose City Council, along with sign maker Roy Rundle, Food Machinery Corp. controller Ben Carter, attorney Albert J. Ruffo, San Jose City Lines mechanic Fred Watson and farmer James Lively. Within days, Police Chief John N. Black and Fire Chief Charles Plummer retired and City Manager Goodwin resigned.

"Then we got to work," Ernie recalls. "The big problem wasn't penny-ante corruption, the big problem was that for years the city hadn't spent a dime to build for the future. We pledged to serve only a single term, to call the shots as we saw them and not to worry about getting re-elected."

Though Ruffo and Watson would run for, and win, subsequent terms, the "Progress" council ran San Jose from 1944 through 1948 and then bowed out of politics. Its achievements are remarkable — and still visible today. They shaped the way San Jose grew. For example:

* The storm water and sanitary sewer systems were separated, paving the way for today's multi-million dollar sewage treatment plant — and high-density urban development.

* Plan lines were adopted for the street widenings and extensions that form the basis for today's traffic grid.

* The right-of-way was pinned down for what was to become Route 17 freeway, the city's main north-south artery.

* Municipal Airport's first runways were opened and commercial air travel became a reality.

* Parking meters (unloved but lucrative) sprang up downtown.

* Land was bought and staff assembled for the first comprehensive parks and recreation program.

* The city administration was professionalized under a first-rate city manager, Orvin W. "Hump" Campbell.

Looking back, Ernie concedes some of the planning may have been short-sighted: "We thought San Jose would have maybe 250,000 population by 1970 (it had 447,025); we didn't foresee how fast and how far we would grow. It's still a pretty town, and I think it always will be. Do you know, even today raccoons come into my backyard? They climb up out of the Coyote Creek, where you can still catch crayfish with bacon on a string . . .

"San Jose has been good to my family; I just want to leave it a little better than I found it."

When Ernie Renzel says it, it doesn't sound corny.

OCTOGENARIAN ERNIE RENZEL STILL LIVES IN SAN JOSE, KEEPS ABREAST OF DOINGS AT CITY HALL AND LUNCHES PERIODICALLY WITH OLD FRIENDS AT THE SAINTE CLAIRE CLUB.

Former San Jose City Manager O. W. "Hump" Campbell, former airport manager Jim Nissen and outgoing commission chairman Marilyn Nyman ham it up with Ernie Renzel on the occasion of a luncheon in his honor celebrating eight years on the Airport Commission. Mercury News photo, June 1977.

San Jose's Biblioteca Is Unique Community Resource

December 12, 1979

We are many and varied in this Santa Clara Valley, and our Hispanic heritage is old and honorable. We all know that.

What many of us in the Anglo community may not know is that our Hispanic heritage is more than historical. It is alive and well and serving us today.

It is a part of Where We Live in ways that sometimes surprise. Take, for example, *Biblioteca Latino Americana.*

Biblioteca is a library, as you might assume from the name. But it is a very special library, one of only two in the entire state, according to Rita Torres, who ought to know.

Biblioteca Latino Americana, at 690 Locust Street, is one of 19 branches in the City of San Jose Public Library system. It is San Jose's Latin-American library. Here, the books in English are kept in the foreign language section.

Other libraries around the state maintain a foreign language section, but only Oakland and San Jose public libraries have branches wholly devoted to Hispanic literature and reference works for children and adults.

Biblioteca's history is short, but its future seems almost limitless. The federal government funded it as an experiment in 1975, but the library didn't open its doors (in the old convent of Sacred Heart Church at Willow and Palm streets) until 1976. The California State Library, which was overseeing the project, wouldn't give the go-ahead until San Jose could find a qualified bilingual librarian. Enter Nora Sepulveda and, later, Rita Torres.

In April 1976, Nora Sepulveda, then a bilingual library clerk, opened *Biblioteca's* doors to the Latinos and Latinas who make up 60 percent of all the residents of the Gardner-Alma neighborhood. In August of that year Rita Torres came aboard as librarian — San Jose's first officially certified bilingual and bicultural librarian. (Nora went on to become San Jose's first bilingual/bicultural children's librarian, working out of the Hillview branch.)

Rita is a native San Josean, born in the Berryessa district 28 years ago. She was a Chicana who

Biblioteca's 13th anniversary party with Jose Luis Orozco, musician and composer. Photo courtesy of Biblioteca.

always loved books. By the time she got to San Jose State University, the federal government was putting money into bilingual programs. "It was fate," says Rita.

It was serendipity for Rita and for San Jose. By the time she was graduated from the university, community pressures for a Spanish-language library had produced the federal funds that got *Biblioteca* started. It needed a bilingual/bicultural librarian. Rita needed a job, and after four separate screening processes, she was interviewed by a panel composed of citizen advisors and Library Department supervisorial personnel. Only then was she offered the job, which she accepted.

We can all be thankful, because Rita has turned *Biblioteca Latino Americana* into a unique community resource. She is quick to point out she didn't do it alone, and she is probably more acutely aware than anyone else of how much more could be done. The library, which is a community center as well as Spanish-language library, could use more room, more books, more of just about everything.

Biblioteca's 7,000 books, 2,500 records and assorted magazines have been lodged since the

first of this year in what used to be the cafeteria of Woodrow Wilson Junior High School at Vine and Locust streets. *Biblioteca* circulates more than 800 of those books and records weekly, and it provides programs and special assistance for an estimated 180 adults and children each week. The two full-time librarians (Rita and Gloria Heinz) and one part-time clerk are kept busy, but it's the nature of that business which makes *Biblioteca* special.

"We're not just a Chicano library," Rita explains. "We're a Latin-American library. We have people come in here from Chile, Guatemala, Nicaragua, almost every Central and South American country, not just Mexico — Spain, too, for that matter."

What do they want? Everything from job-related how-to-material and tracts on health and hygiene to escapist reading — including Caballero, the Spanish-language best-of-Playboy. "That was a high rip-off item," Rita recalls, "until we started keeping it behind the librarian's counter."

Not surprisingly, *Biblioteca* plays a big role in ushering the bilingual students from Washington and Gardner schools into full familiarization

28

with the English language; the transition usually takes place in the fifth or sixth grades, says Rita.

Finally, and perhaps most surprising of all, *Biblioteca* is used intensively by segments of San Jose's Anglo community, too. Theater and dance students from San Jose State come by for pictorially accurate data on Hispanic costumes. Similarly, students of everything from classical guitar to Iberian furniture use *Biblioteca* as a handy reference, and Anglos who want to retain their fluency in Spanish come in just to talk.

We may have different heritages, but we're all one people. If you doubt that, go ask Rita Torres.

THE BIBLIOTECA, STILL LODGED IN ITS WILSON JUNIOR HIGH QUARTERS, IS BURSTING AT THE SEAMS WITH ALMOST 25,000 VOLUMES, OUT 2,000 RECORDS AND ALMOST 600 AUDIO CASSETTES. RITA TORRES NOW RUNS THE FOREIGN LANGUAGE DESK AT THE MAIN SAN JOSE LIBRARY, WHILE GLORIA HEINZ IS HEAD LIBRARIAN AT THE PEARL AVENUE BRANCH. NORA SEPULVEDA CONTE IS AT THE HILLVIEW LIBRARY. BIBLIOTECA'S LIBRARIAN TODAY IS LINDA MENDEZ-ORTIZ.

From San Jose to America's Servicemen a Gift of the Heart

December 19, 1979

This is a slightly different kind of Christmas story. It's about giving, which is traditional enough at this time of year, but this story is about a town that gave of itself, not in a single, magnificent burst of generosity, but quietly and steadily for 35 years.

It gave, in fact, until there was no further reason to give. I'm talking about San Jose, and about some very special men and women who helped make this a giving, welcoming place.

The story starts the summer before Pearl Harbor. Everybody knew war was coming. We didn't know when, or where, but we knew Congress hadn't extended the draft as a way to fight unemployment. The Army was buying up chunks of the Central Coast for training centers — infantry at Camp (later Fort) Ord near Monterey, coast artillery at Camp McQuaide near Watsonville. There was even an inter-service scrap between the Army and Navy for the use of Moffett Field. (The Army won for a time, but the Navy had staying power; it got the place back and still has it.)

We could tell, that summer of 1941, it would not be long before large numbers of soldiers, sailors and airmen began passing through San Jose.

Older men, some of whom had experienced war before, sensed the job that needed to be done — men such as Jay McCabe, who ran the Civic Auditorium, Russ Pettit of the Chamber of Commerce, clothiers Phil Hammer and Leland Prussia, and Jose Levitt, later to become a radio magnate. They understood the need for an off-duty haven where a soldier or sailor could see and touch and smell the civilian world of yesterday and prepare himself emotionally for the ordeal of tomorrow.

The United Service Organizations was about to come to San Jose. There was an ideal site for a USO center, City Hall Plaza in downtown San Jose, but the city had no money for a building. Neither did the USO. That didn't stop the city's business community and its laboring men. With the organizing help of McCabe et al., they scrounged the materials and got to work.

On August 16, 1941, at 7 a.m., 160 skilled

30

USO Hut in City Plaza. San Jose Historical Museum collections.

tradesmen — carpenters, plumbers, roofers, painters, electricians — turned to. It was a typically hot San Jose August, and the sweat flowed; but only once did the 160 stop for longer than 30 seconds. That was at 8 a.m., when they laid down their tools for a brief flag-raising and dedication ceremony. The carpenters on the roof couldn't stand at attention, but they held their hats over their hearts as the flag went up.

Army cooks from Moffett Field served them from field kitchens set up in the plaza. By 8:24 p.m. the 160 unpaid volunteers had turned $4,500 worth of donated construction materials into an L-shaped structure, 20 x 30 feet in one wing and 16 x 40 feet in the other. San Jose's USO Hut was born. It was a gift from start to finish; even the plans were donated by architect Charles McKenzie.

Tradition has it that the USO Hut was built in a single day, but that's not wholly accurate. The structure was raised and finished in one day, but a crew of carpenters and cement masons spent August 15 placing mudsills and laying the floor. They also shaped up half the framing.

One day, two days, who's counting? It was a beautiful gift, and 113 days later, on December 7,

1941, the Empire of Japan guaranteed the San Jose USO Hut a long run. The real giving was about to begin.

No memoir of the USO Hut, abandoned and partially demolished in 1974 and finally torn down in 1976, would be complete without mention of Rosa and David Roy and San Jose's Jewish community.

On that first wartime Christmas, Dr. and Mrs. David Roy and a dozen or so other members of Temple Emanu-El, then the only temple in town, volunteered to prepare and serve a traditional Christmas dinner to the servicemen at the USO Hut. The event was such a success the Jewish community turned it into a tradition that lasted 30 years.

As Dr. Roy, a San Jose chiropractor, recalls, "We wanted to free our Christian neighbors to celebrate their holiest day at home with their families and in their churches. We were happy to do it."

You'll go a long way to find a more practical demonstration of inter-faith brotherhood.

From 1941 until 1976, when it folded for good, the San Jose USO was a home away from home for more than one million American servicemen. They played games, ate, danced with the local girls (and married some of them), wrote letters home and tried to recapture a sense of what life was like Before.

But when the conscript army died, the USO died with it. Career soldiers with money in their pockets don't need and don't frequent USO Huts. That's how Louis Rossi, who served as president of the San Jose USO for 25 years, explains what

happened.

In 1974, with attendance way down, the USO moved out of the Hut and into a city-owned building at 245 Carlyle Street. In 1975, the United Way chopped its contribution to $12,000 for the year, and on January 12, 1976, the San Jose USO passed into history.

It was a wonderful gift while it lasted, and it lasted as long as it was needed.

For Years He Wore Two Hats:
Union Organizer and Lobbyist

December 26, 1979

Dr. Ernesto Galarza is 74 now and retired from the farm labor wars that absorbed his attention for nearly two decades. He insists, with characteristic but unjustified modesty, that he had little to do with making San Jose the place it is today.

In a narrow geographical sense, he is right; but in the broader perspective he has had, and continues to have, a significant impact on how, if not where, we live.

Ernesto and Mae Galarza live today in a small, blue house on a shady Willow Glen side street. The Ibero-American decorations are understated but impressive. The place is warm and welcoming, like the people who live in it.

To understand Ernie Galarza you have to go back to 1912. He was 5, and revolution was sweeping across Mexico. The older male Galarzas were section hands for the Southern Pacific railroad, which was then extending its lines down the west coast of Mexico.

"The railroad and the instability of the revolution got to Mazatlan about the same time," he recalls. "The railroad made up a refugee train, and soldiers guarded it to the border at Nogales. My mother and I were on it, and the first thing she asked for when we crossed into Arizona was, 'Where is the school?' Whenever we moved, that was what she asked for first."

Ultimately, the Galarzas settled in Sacramento, where Mrs. Galarza immediately located the school and Ernesto learned English and the ways of American capitalism hawking the *Sacramento Bee* on the city's downtown streets. It was an early introduction to a lifetime of labor and intellectual curiosity. (By 1944, he had earned a doctorate in history and political science, from Columbia University.)

He and Mae, a graduate of San Jose State College, moved to San Jose in 1947. She taught; he helped organize, and later served as director of research and education for the AFL's fledgling effort to unionize the fields — the National Farm Workers Union.

"We needed a home base," Galarza recalls, "and San Jose was ideally situated. From here you can keep track of the two currents of northward

Mexican migration, the one up the coast from San Diego, the other through the Imperial and Central Valleys to Marysville and Yuba City."

There was good reason to keep track of the currents; the presence of *braceros,* or contract laborers from Mexico made it exceedingly difficult to unionize farm workers. Where the union got a toehold, or seemed about to get one, the grower would fire his workers and apply for a permit to import *braceros.* They had little incentive to join the NFWU because their stay here was to be temporary. Also it was tenuous. Most growers made it clear that joining the union was equivalent to asking for a bus ticket back to Mexico.

Consequently, what happened to the NFWU isn't surprising. It folded in 1964, its charter absorbed by the Butchers' Union. At the height of its influence, the NFWU boasted about 4,000 members in 20 locals statewide. The union was down to six locals and barely 200 members when it went out of business. A defeat for Ernesto

Ernesto Galarza, 1961. Mercury News photo.

Galarza and the cause of a living wage for farm workers? Not really.

For years, Ernesto Galarza had worn two hats, union organizer and lobbyist against the iniquities of the *bracero* program. His credentials for both jobs were impeccable.

In the late '30s and early '40s he spent 10 years on the staff of the Pan-American Union in Washington, building contacts on both sides of the border. He wrote and lectured. He testified before assorted agencies of government in Washington and Mexico City. Always the message was the same: The *bracero* program exploits Mexicans and depresses living standards for Americans.

It was a water-on-stone strategy, and it worked —but too late to save the NFWU. However, by the time the *bracero* program was junked formally in 1963, another San Josean, Cesar Chavez, was ready to move into the vacuum. Today's United Farm Workers union, founded and still led by Chavez, is the lineal descendant and beneficiary of Ernesto Galarza's pioneering.

But what has Dr. Galarza done to keep busy since getting out of the union business? Well, in 1963 he served as chief labor consultant to the Education and Labor Committee of the House of Representatives. He was scholar-in-residence at San Jose State University in 1973.

Perhaps most interesting of all, he planned, authored, and helped illustrate a dozen children's books, in both Spanish and English. They served as the nucleus of a bilingual/bicultural teacher-training program that operated in Santa Clara County until recently. Ten of the 12 *mini-libros* have been accepted as elementary textbooks by the state of California.

In his mind's ear, Ernie Galarza seems still to be hearing his mother's question: "Where is the school?"

ERNESTO GALARZA DIED IN JUNE, 1984 BUT HE REMAINS A PRESENCE IN THE COMMUNITY. HIS PAPERS, OR MOST OF THEM, ARE HOUSED IN THE SPECIAL COLLECTIONS DIVISION OF THE STANFORD UNIVERSITY LIBRARY. PROFESSOR CARLOS MUNOZ, OF U.C. BERKELEY, IS WORKING ON GALARZA'S BIOGRAPHY,

AND BOTH STANFORD AND SAN JOSE STATE UNIVERSITIES OFFER ANNUAL SCHOLARSHIPS IN HIS NAME, ACCORDING TO HIS WIDOW, MAE, WHO STILL LIVES IN SAN JOSE. IN 1986, OCCIDENTAL COLLEGE, GALARZA'S ALMA MATER, DEVOTED ONE NIGHT OF ITS CENTENNIAL CELEBRATION TO THE ERNESTO GALARZA LEGACY.

Farm laborers harvesting field crops in Santa Clara County, c. 1970. Mercury News photo.

'Holy City' is a Tattered
Monument to Eccentricity

January 2, 1980

San Jose has never won renown as the kook capital of California, but we've had our share of eccentrics — Sarah Winchester of Mystery House fame comes most readily to mind.

Eccentrics are worth passing mention in any examination of a community because they add spice and a hint of the ultimate possibilities of individualism. They are our other selves, for better or for worse.

No exploration of San Jose area eccentrics would be complete without recalling "Father" William Edward Riker, founder of the "Perfect Christian Divine Way" and for years the first Citizen of Holy City in the Santa Cruz mountains south of Los Gatos.

Hardly anybody remembers Holy City anymore. There's no reason they should. It's a ghost town now, reachable only with some difficulty (take the Redwood Estates exit from Highway 17). I was reminded of "Father Riker" and Holy City the other day when a letter arrived from Lou Murphy, a technical editor with Lockheed

Missiles & Space Co. in Sunnyvale.

Lou's Personal View of Where We Live encompasses Holy City where, from 1953 through 1955, he and Charles Norman co-published a literary quarterly, the *Mountain Echo*. Lou and Charlie printed it in the Holy City Print Shop, about the last surviving commercial venture of what was once a religious commune of some novelty.

Riker, whom Lou recalls vividly, was a third-grade dropout who left his home in the San Joaquin Valley town of Oakdale to make his way as a necktie salesman in San Francisco. Neckties didn't pay, but Riker, who by then was studying mysticism and metaphysics, found that palm reading and a fake mind-reading act did.

Emboldened by success, he conferred on himself the title of "The Comforter" and began preaching salvation through white supremacy. By 1914 Riker had gathered a number of apostles as well as a drayage company in San Francisco, and in 1918 he incorporated the "Perfect Christian Divine Way." A year later he relocated his flock of 13 disciples on 200 acres along the old Santa Cruz highway. Holy City was born; its business build-

Holy City, high up in the Santa Cruz mountains, 17 miles from San Jose. Partly hidden by trees on the left is Father Riker's home. Mercury News photo, 1938.

ings — a garage, service station, barber shop, print shop, hotel, radio station, general store and restaurant — were built from material salvaged by Riker from razed San Francisco homes.

For years, Holy City thrived on the tourist trade. You couldn't drive to the coast without passing through and Riker's gingerbread architecture and outrageous pseudo-religious huckstering turned that section of the Santa Cruz mountains into a Depression-era Disneyland.

By 1953, though, Holy City and "Father" Riker were passe. But let Lou Murphy tell about it.

"When I was there, there were about 12 members of the sect left — then in their 60s, 70s, and 80s. They lived in separate houses but shared a community dining room. Jim Edmonson ran the garage, Emil Reichsteiner, the town barber, was 76. Joseph Albert, the youngest member at 61, was for 30 years Holy City business manager. Later, as bartender, he was shot and robbed.

"But I knew Stephen 'Rosie' Rozum best. He was a former Hindu monk who trained for the Catholic priesthood in Poland and joined Riker in 1916. He was in his 60s in 1953. A slim, energetic man, he had the only new car in Holy City and the most profitable business in town, the Holy City Print Shop. His shop was spacious and well-equipped, and in exchange for free rent and the use of his equipment to print the *Mountain Echo,* we helped him hand-set ads from the California job case, run off business cards on the job press and sweep the shop . . .

"Rosie also printed the cult's religious tracts, one of which was entitled *The Book of Books That Surely Sizzles With the Final Wisdom of God.*

"Riker, four times candidate for governor of California, had a reported income of $100,000 a year. He would visit us often in the print shop, and we also sat with him occasionally in his imposing home on the hill across the road while he propounded his latest philosophy. About that time he was insisting he had the secret of eternal life. 'You watch,' he'd say. 'Every day I'm going to get younger and younger.'

"But he didn't. He was 80 then, and he died at age 96 in Agnews State Hospital. He made the news columns one last time before going to whatever eternal reward awaited him: He converted to Catholicism in a highly publicized ceremony.

"They're all dead now, and Holy City has all but been bulldozed from the landscape. Edmonson's garage tilts crazily on its pilings, the roof caved in from age and fire. Riker's house still stands on the knoll, and someone seems to be living in it. The row of two-story buildings that houses the print shop, post office, grocery store and bar have burned to the ground, and the ornate semi-religious signs are gone. But there is still a quiet beauty about the place, marred only by the box-like wooden structure that houses the Holy City Post Office.

"We built apace during those years; the orchards, it seemed, had to go. But now I sense a change; perhaps it's a wish. The builders have

Fr. William E. Riker. Mercury news photo.

had their day, and it's time to pause, to recoup. Let Nature temper the violence done to the land. Let the air clear. Make the valley green again."

Nobody'll argue with that, Lou.

San Jose's First Doctor Caught Gold Fever in Rush of '48

January 16, 1980

Dr. Benjamin Cory, the first physician to settle in the pueblo de San Jose (in 1847), died here on this date in 1896 and was buried in the Pioneers Section of Oak Hill Memorial Park.

He is probably spinning in that grave today.

Dr. Cory was many things to many men: doctor, singer (he favored hymns), school trustee, city councilman, state assemblyman, first city health officer (unofficial), county physician (official) and civic leader.

He and 18 other San Joseans chipped in $34,000 to build the first state Capitol in San Jose, and he was instrumental in building the first County Hospital, in 1875, on the site where Valley Medical Center now stands.

But Dr. Cory was something more. He was an Argonaut, an authentic victim of the gold fever that afflicted *Californios* in 1848 and spread eastward the following year.

Ben Cory dropped his San Jose practice twice, making trips to the diggings in 1848 and 1849. He enjoyed modest success (about $4,000 worth), but with gold selling today for more than $600 an ounce, Dr. Ben would surely climb out of that grave if he could.

I say that advisedly. On November 6, 1848, Dr. Benjamin Cory wrote a letter to his brother, Dr. Andrew Jackson Cory, of Ohio, urging him to come West. The California brother wrote from Gold Placero, a Mother Lode locale now lost to history; it could have been on the banks of any creek between Mariposa and Nevada City in the foothills of the Sierra Nevada mountains. And Ben was pitching hard to get Andy to join him.

The fascinating letter helps turn a legend into a human being. I am indebted to an old and dear friend, Dr. Milton J. Chatton, county medical society historian and a former director of VMC, who has the original Cory letter. Here are some excerpts:

"...This is the richest gold country on the face of the globe. Gold almost looks to me like a worthless toy — I have seen such vast quantities of it. A man, here in the mountains, who has not 10 or 20 pounds of it is looked upon as a poverty-stricken man. I think the gold here is quite pure;

it must be worth at a mint some $18 or $19 an ounce...The first month I was in the mines, myself and partner dug out $3,000 apiece, calling each ounce $16. The diggings then became poor (and) a man had to work hard all day for only an ounce or two..."

Nonetheless, Dr. Ben expressed confidence that he would clear $100,000 in three years, "if my days in comfort and in dispensing blessings upon those poor mortals whom I have often wished to assist, but could not for want of means..."

A. J. Cory, M.D., 1873. W. W. Wright, photographer. San Jose Historical Museum collections.

Benjamin Cory, M.D., 1867. J. H. Heering photographer. San Jose Historical Museum collections.

In the meantime, however, Dr. Ben had a problem. Those "poor mortals" weren't willing to wait for him to get comfortable.

"I am sorry, dear brother," Ben lamented to Andy, "that I ever had 'Dr.' stuck to my name. It is more trouble than profit. I am vexed to death. I tell people I can get more gold in the mountains by digging and trading than my conscience will permit. I tell them that I have quit the practice of medicine; I am occupied with other pursuits

more congenial to my feelings. But it all does no good; when a man *begs* of me to go see his friend, I cannot but go.

"At first here in the mountains I charged $8 a visit if the patient was near, and very high mileage if he was at a distance. But you know how it is everywhere; people do not like to pay a doctor bill, and I am a poor collector. Three-fourths went away to other gold diggings without calling on me...

"But I cannot quit practicing. I tried another plan. I practiced without charging a cent. I showed every applicant that I went with extreme reluctance. I attended with negligence, told the friends of the patient that I was no longer a physician, that I shouldered no responsibility etc. But this would not do. I was pestered more than ever.

"I have now determined on another plan. I shall always have a quantity of medicine with me, shall attend patients when I have time and *charge abundantly*. I will visit no patient for less than an ounce of gold, will ride no where to see the sick for less than half an ounce, unless it is a rare case — a case of poverty."

That was the wind-up. Then Dr. Ben delivered the pitch.

"Tell my relatives," he writes, " that they must not be angry with me when I urge you to come to this country; you are quite young, I know, but you have a good education and can thrive in this country. There is no country on the face of the earth where a fortune can be made so easily as in California...Come to California immediately!

Come on the steamer by way of Panama. You can get here in 30 or 40 days, and what is that. Come and I will be a *good brother* to you. You need not have a cent of money when you land, for I will divide generously with you, and take you as full partner in my business..."

And that's the way it happened. Both doctors lived out their lives here, tending the sick and injured and nursing San Jose from Mexican pueblo to American city. The gold petered out, but the doctors Cory died rich in finer coin — love and honors.

Ray Blackmore:
Cop and 'Politician' for 42 Years

January 23, 1980

John Raymond Blackmore, "Ray" to his friends, worked his way up through the ranks of the San Jose Police Department to become chief on March 1, 1947. The day he was promoted was nearly his last.

"Three detectives, myself included, were called to this house to arrest a rape suspect," Ray recalled the other day.

"I knocked on the door, and the guy answered with a 12-gauge shotgun blast through the woodwork. I went over the porch rail and landed in a blackberry bush. The lady who had called us crept over to me and said, 'Mister, that man's crazy.' I told her I just figured that out."

Ultimately, the suspected rapist was talked into surrendering, and nobody got hurt. Still, it was one of an even dozen times that Ray Blackmore cheated death in the line of duty.

As Ray remembers it, "I got to City Hall that evening and found I had been named chief of police. It was quite a day."

It was also a watershed of sorts.

Ray Blackmore was hired as a police patrolman in the spring of 1929 because he was a hot prospect for the departmental baseball team. Charlie Bigley, ambulance-operator-cum-political-boss, liked Ray's looks. City Manager Clarence B. Goodwin didn't. He thought Ray, at 5-foot-7 inches, was too short. Politics being what it was in those days, Bigley prevailed.

Ray was 21 then and the principal support of his widowed mother. He was 17 when he dropped out of San Jose High School just short of graduation in order to go to work. He boxed a bit, worked in a canning machinery factory, played semi-pro baseball. The police appointment, which began as just another job, became a passion. "I found I liked chasing burglars," is the way Ray puts it today.

He liked it so well he stayed on for 42 years, the last of them as chief. He said San Jose grew from a market town to a sophisticated industrial metropolis, and he helped shape a significant part of that growth.

If Ray was lucky to have found his niche in 1929, San Jose was equally lucky. "I was never

Ray Blackmore, 1975. Mercury News photo

any genius," he says, "but I always was willing to work."

He was always willing to learn, too. In 1943, he flunked the examination for the newly created post of chief of detectives. So did every other detective sergeant. Ray got mad — "at myself" — he recalls now, and enlisted the aid of an attorney friend who coached him for the re-examination. Ray passed the next time around.

By 1947, a reform City Council had broken Bigley's political grip and ousted Goodwin, and Ray Blackmore, the 1929 patronage cop (who nonetheless had passed the civil service examination for patrolman), went on to lay the groundwork for today's modern professional force.

The San Jose Police Department numbered approximately 100 officers on March 1, 1947. It had grown to 1,200 men and women by the time Ray Blackmore retired, on May 17, 1971. By then, too, patronage was out; education was in. Ray insisted rookies have at least two years of college. More was encouraged. And the high school dropout chief had joined the faculty of San Jose State

College, where he taught police administration part-time for a dozen years.

After 1947, the old order, indeed, yielded place to the new. Ray Blackmore pursued fewer burglars and more good works. He became a politician in the best sense of that word. Ray had (and still has) the knack of getting people to work together.

Over the years Ray has headed countless fund-raising committees — for the YMCA, the YWCA, Goodwill Industries, hospitals; you name it; he's worked for it. The $525,000 Police Activities League sports complex in East San Jose is another of his monuments.

Ray's tireless organizing and cajoling helped persuade San Jose and Santa Clara County voters to approve more than $239 million in construction bonds in the 1950s and 1960s. Those bonds bought the infrastructure of today's community — a modern sewer system and sewage treatment plant, firehouses, libraries, a new City Hall and the first consolidated city-county jail.

Characteristically, Ray Blackmore didn't retire to a rocking chair in 1971. He organized a crime prevention program for the county's construction industry, helped found the Santa Clara County Association for Good Government and took over community relations chores for Oak Hill Memorial Park.

An alert 73 (he stays fit with handball), Ray took a stab the other day at summing up his times and his hometown. It's a mixed judgment.

"We grew so rapidly, and on balance so well, after World War II," he mused, "because a lot of people were willing to work for what they saw as the common good. They trusted government and cooperated with it.

"We're not so trustful now, and it's harder to get things done. Also it takes longer. Somewhere along the line, the old partnership broke down, but that doesn't mean we can't or won't revive it. We just have to remember this is our home. It can be as good or as bad as we want to make it."

Right on, Native Son.

RAY BLACKMORE DIED ON NOVEMBER 22, 1988.

She Didn't Know Anything About Braille but She Learned

January 30, 1980

"Honey, my friends all say, 'look out for Sylvia, if you're her friend, she'll put you to work.' They've been saying that for as long as I can remember, and I guess they're right."

That's one of Sylvia Cassell's throw-away lines. She tossed it over her shoulder the other day as we were leaving the Santa Clara Valley Blind Center, 101 N. Bascom Avenue.

It's true, too. People fall over themselves to work for Sylvia because only an insensitive clod could resist her special blend of southern charm and Yankee practicality. For the past 24 years she's been using both to open up the world to the blind.

More than 2,000 blind youngsters in Santa Clara County have been able to go to neighborhood schools with their sighted classmates because of Sylvia and her friends. In addition, they have helped blind men and women in 40 other states learn how to function more fully in the world, at a cost to the taxpayers of precisely nothing.

Sylvia Cassell is, and for almost a quarter-century has been, head of Santa Clara County's Sixth District PTA Braille Transcription Project. She and her transcribers, about 125 of them at the moment, create books blind people can read by passing their fingers over raised dots. Over the years, these unpaid volunteers have amassed a 10,000-volume Braille library at the Blind Center, and they are constantly adding to it. In addition, they fill special requests — playing cards, cookbooks ("Beyond TV Dinners" is a favorite), exit signs in nursing homes, personnel testing materials for industry. One elderly woman wanted her will Brailled, so she could be sure her last wishes were recorded properly.

And it's all a labor of love. Sylvia and her transcribers work for free. Donations, to the PTA, to other service organizations and to the project directly, pay for the materials.

If special people build special communities, Sylvia Cassell has to be considered one of San Jose's most valuable natural resources.

Born in Atlanta, Georgia, 65 years ago, Sylvia was reared in the south (Atlanta and Birmingham, Alabama) and educated there and in New York City. She arrived here in 1934 with her parents, Col. and Mrs. D. I. Brosseau. The colonel, in civilian life a marketing specialist and consultant, took one look at San Jose and settled down. Sylvia was then 20, a petite bundle of energy given to wearing camellias in her brunette hair (she still does). Within two years she had met and married Dr. Irving Cassell, an eye, ear, nose and throat specialist.

A proper Briton, the Manchester-born Dr. Cassell built a home for his bride, at 1634 Shasta Avenue, before the wedding. The newlyweds moved in directly after the honeymoon, in the summer of 1936, and spent the rest of their married life there. Dr. Cassell died in the house in 1974 after a long illness. He was 72.

Sylvia and Irving (whom she still calls "my sweetheart") reared two children, Beverly and David, on Shasta Avenue, and it was the children who indirectly propelled Sylvia into the blind transcription project. That happened in 1956. Sylvia recalls it thus:

"Beverly was 18 and David was 16 then, but I was still in the PTA. I'd been a Cub Scout den mother and a Girl Scout leader, and I'd packed

Sylvia Cassell, 1983. Photo courtesy of Beverly Cassell Domenech.

all that up, but I was never able to get out of the PTA. I don't think anybody is ever allowed to quit the PTA.

"Dr. Hubbard (then county superintendent of schools) came to us one day and said there were 18 blind children who couldn't go to regular school because there weren't enough supplementary texts in Braille for the little ones, and there weren't any books at all for the high school kids. He wanted to know could we help. I didn't know anything about Braille, but I figured, shoot, I could learn."

The San Jose Adult Education program gave her a classroom, and a blind social worker named Edwin Lanini gave her and her PTA volunteers their first lessons in Braille. Ed had to use beans to simulate the raised-dot characters because there was no better equipment available.

The program has been growing since. Sylvia still trains transcribers and works two days a week at the Blind Center. After 24 years, the project's library and transcription service have become a national resource, filling requests from 40 to 50 states. Alaska and Hawaii have asked Sylvia to set up similar programs for them, and she's obliged.

That's why Sylvia Cassell has a ton of plaques and award certificates squirreled away in the Shasta Avenue house, and that's why there's a Sylvia Cassell School in the Alum Rock School District.

She's earned the honors, but she's not impressed by them. As we parted the other day, she gave me a hug and flashed that pixy grin of hers. "Honey," she purred, "it's what you do in life that's important, not what people say about you."

Is it any wonder she's had four proposals of marriage since Irving died?

SYLVIA HAS RETIRED AS CHAIRMAN OF THE BLIND CENTER, INC. OF SANTA CLARA VALLEY AFTER 30 YEARS WITH THE ORGANIZATION, BUT STILL SERVES AS A CONSULTANT" WHICH MEANS I DON'T HAVE SO MANY HEADACHES," SHE EXPLAINS. STILL ACTIVE IN TRANSCRIBING FOR THE BLIND, SYLVIA CONDUCTED A BRAILLE WORKSHOP IN SWEDEN THIS PAST JUNE (1989).

Hump Campbell Recalls Days as City Manager

February 6, 1980

Orvin W. "Hump" Campbell is a short, rotund man to whom the years have been kind. At 74, his sense of humor is as keen as ever, and he still refuses to waste time on pretense or self-deception. All told, that's a pretty good prescription for longevity.

Hump Campbell was among us, officially, for less than four years, from June 10, 1946 until January 31, 1950, but the timing of his stay and the strength of his personality played a significant part in shaping San Jose as we know it. If you like the place, you can thank Hump, at least a little. If you don't like what you see, don't blame Campbell. Had he stayed longer, things might have been different.

There are those who argue O. W. Campbell was the best city manager San Jose ever had, and they will get no argument from me on that score. Hump reorganized the city administration to emphasize competence over politics. He built new firehouses, widened and improved major streets and laid the groundwork for today's major

Orvin W. "Hump" Campbell, 1949. Mercury News photo.

Municipal Airport and multi-stage sewage treatment plant.

He was a professional. He knew what a city needs to function efficiently, and he knew how

46

to get it. He could be demanding, of himself and of others, and he was uncompromisingly honest.

But the thing I always liked best about Hump Campbell was his ability to tell a good story, to make a point with verve and humor. Hump, who was in town last week to renew old acquaintances, hasn't lost the knack.

The conversation turned — as such conversations will — to past triumphs, to defeats and turning points. I recalled how Hump had been wooed by the cities of Berkeley, Pasadena and Stockton and by Alameda and Santa Clara counties before he was finally lured to the greener pastures and greater glories of San Diego. The mention of Stockton, where years before Hump had designed the city's first civil service system, got him started on one of his better stories:

"You remember, of course (but, of course, I didn't) that Stockton was in the middle of a nasty, lurid recall fight at that time. The faction trying to oust the city council old guard offered me the city manager's job, and I told them to ask me again if they got elected."

(The temptation to return to Stockton may have been strong; Hump was born in nearby Lodi.)

"Well," Hump continued, "came the election and some of the recall people were elected and some of the old guard were retained. It had been an ugly fight, and the outcome left Stockton in a touchy situation.

"The new — and very mixed — council asked me to come over for a talk. We danced around for awhile, with nobody willing to come right out and ask me what I'd put up with if I took the job.

Lustily singing, left to right, standing: Ben Carter, James Lively and Ernest Renzel, Jr. Seated: Roy Rundle, O. W. "Hump" Campbell, and Fred Watson. The occasion was a reunion of members of the San Jose City Council who had served with City Manager Campbell. Mercury News photo.

It was pretty clear this could go on forever, so I figured it was time to get to the point.

"Gentlemen", I told them, "I've been following your recall closely in the papers, and if even half of what I read is true, I can tell you one thing. If I come to work here, at least one man in this room is going to jail."

Hump didn't get the job.

The whole point, of course, is that he didn't want it with strings attached. Hump is a fighter, but he's no trimmer. He could also play political games with the best of them.

One of the first serious morale problems Hump faced as San Jose city manager concerned the Fire Department. Part of the trouble was resentment of the new chief, Lester O'Brien, by some of the senior officers who fancied themselves in the chief's helmet; part stemmed from incipient unionization of the firefighters.

Hump's solution was ingenious, if devious. He had O'Brien resign.

Les handed in a letter of resignation (which Hump had no intention of accepting) and went into seclusion "for a rest on doctor's orders." Actually, Les and his wife went to their Santa Cruz beach house and took the telephone off the hook.

Hump huffed and puffed, in the press and in City Hall staff meetings, about "getting to the bottom of all these rumors about the chief...If anybody has any charges to bring, I want them, and I want them now, in detail and in the open."

The anti-O'Brien campaign collapsed, and Les remained fire chief until he retired — years after Hump had departed to San Diego and then to Miami, where he was the first executive officer of Dade County's metropolitan government. I imagine he operated there pretty much the same way he did here, with no nonsense but a twinkle in his eye.

Campbell's retired now, lives up the coast in Rossmoor. He rolls his own cigarettes and alternates naps and martinis "for fun," and his explanation of this leisure-time preference is pure Hump:

"Whaddya expect? I never had time to learn golf."

HUMP CAMPBELL DIED IN HIS RETIREMENT HOME, IN WALNUT CREEK, IN DECEMBER 1986 AT THE AGE OF 80.

Goosetown

February 20, 1980

Dr. Dan C. Lopez is a professor of industrial arts at San Jose State University, and he lives in the comfort of Saratoga now. But he grew up in "Goosetown," as the portion of San Jose west of Almaden Avenue was known before World War II.

Almaden was formally designated Orchard Street then, and when Dr. Lopez was coming to maturity there in the mid-1920s the area was home to a flourishing Italian community, leavened with a dusting of other minority groups. It was also the rumored enclave of a gang of ruffians known locally as "Ali Baba and the 40 Thieves," but that isn't what the good doctor recalls most vividly about the district.

Most of all, he remembers Dimas. Herewith, Dr. Lopez:

"The one unforgettable character of 'Goosetown' I knew as a boy was Dimas, an itinerant tinsmith of Mexican birth. Everybody in Cottage Grove, and along Almaden Road and up Orchard Street as far as Grant Street (where 280 crosses now) knew him. He was a Charlie Chaplin-like little man, with baggy trousers, worn shoes and a porkpie hat, and he was never seen without his charcoal brazier and a few hand tools characteristic of his trade, or *oficio.*"

"Dimas was born in Guadalajara, Jalisco, where his father owned a successful *taller* or shop. The lad was apprenticed to his father as a tinsmith, and he might have passed his life in Guadalajara if it hadn't been for The Revolution. Dimas became enamored of the cause espoused by a string of Mexican presidents: Porfirio Diaz, Francisco Madero, Victoriano Huerta and Venustiano Carranza. Central to the hopes of each of these was the bandit Francisco "Pancho" Villa. Alas for poor Dimas, he threw in with Villa and was forced, ultimately, to flee for his life.

The way Dimas always told it, he was enroute to be shot when he jumped train somewhere in the wilds of Sonora. And he would have died in the Sonoran desert, too, he always maintained, except that he was befriended by a *curandera*, whose folk medicine and good cooking nursed him back to health.

"In time he made his way to the border and into California. He didn't stop running until he arrived in Hacienda, a tiny village adjacent to the New Almaden quicksilver mines. Dimas had found his new home.

"In Hacienda, he found countrymen and an opportunity to practice his trade. He mined and repaired pots and pans and made custom utensils for the inhabitants of both Englishtown and Spanishtown. But the mines petered out eventually and Dimas, like many of the miners, moved to San Jose.

"He had no family and, literally, no home. He bedded down in abandoned houses and in rooms provided by friends, but he never had a permanent address. He was a perpetual wanderer in the Greater Goosetown complex. Whenever he stopped to mend utensils or craft a pot or pan, he was fed by the *patron* of the moment. He was gentle, always gallant to the ladies, and there wasn't a youngster or dog in Goosetown that didn't know Dimas by name and scent.

"More than once during Prohibition, Dimas would disappear for a week at a time. Later he told us bootleggers held him captive on a remote ranch while he repaired their still and bottling equipment. Nor were they the only ones to drag a command performance out of him.

"Dimas was not a wino as we know winos today, but he could — and did — drink a lot. That's when the San Jose police and/or the sheriff would pick him up and keep him until the jail's pots, pans and other kitchen equipment were restored to working order. Then Dimas would be turned loose, with some clean clothes and a few dollars for his work.

"Old age and senility closed in on Dimas about the time World War II closed in on the rest of us. He was hit by a car one night while trying to cross his beloved Orchard Street; it was raining hard, and the driver couldn't see the small, bent figure leaning into the storm. Dimas lingered on for a time, in the County Hospital, and then he died. Tradition has it the residents of Goosetown saw to his burial in Potter's Field. I don't know.

"I do know that when Dimas died he put a period to a special era in San Jose's history, an era when many of us spelled home 'Goosetown.'"

March 19, 1980

George Long was born in San Jose 72 years ago and grew up close by, but not precisely within the confines of "Goosetown." It was, he recalls, a place of distinctive sights, smells and denizens that never failed to fascinate.

That is what moved George, now retired and living in the Santa Cruz area, to drop us a line the other day. He had just read Dr. Dan C. Lopez's recollections of Dimas, the itinerant Mexican tinsmith who lived and died, quit literally, on the streets of Goosetown.

"I would add one minor detail," George wrote, "to the part about Dimas being kidnapped periodically by bootleggers...As I heard the story, the people he was dealing with weren't the most trusting individuals in the valley. So, when they picked up Dimas, usually after dark, he was blindfolded as soon as his bottom hit the seat of their car. When they finished with him, they blindfolded him again for the trip home..."

George went on:

"As a kid I was always given to understand that the eastern edge of Goosetown was Orchard Avenue. The southern boundary would be somewhere along a line paralleling what is today West Alma Street. The western edge was easy to pinpoint; it was the Guadalupe Creek. Now, while the northern boundary might be open to debate, I was always told it lay along Grant Street.

"The southern boundary couldn't be extended too far south because then you ran into the Cottage Grove people, who were fiercely independent. And I doubt that the northern edge of Goosetown went much beyond Grant Street; after that you began to run into a different class of people, too . . ."

George then offered a Goosetown vignette of his own. It has everything — patriotism, pathos, humor, mystery. The time was 1918; the United States was on its way to winning World War I. Let George take it from there:

"I couldn't have been over 10 years old at the time, and like all kids of that age I was crazy for ice cream. In those days, Goosetown had its own special ice-cream vendor. He was an old Italian

50

High water from Canoas Creek on Viola Avenue near Orchard street, San Jose, 1911. San Jose Historical Museum collections.

gentleman who drove his horse and wagon through the area almost every day, selling ice cream cones out of an insulated box on the back of the wagon.

"Usually, he'd work his way north on Orchard Street, then swing east on Oak Street until he reached South First Street, where he'd turn left and head uptown. His horse was a nondescript reddish brown, and his wagon always needed a coat of paint.

"You can imagine, then, the double-takes he inspired early on the afternoon of July 4, 1918, when we kids caught sight of him. He was sitting bolt upright on the driver's seat, proud as a peacock, head up, chin jutting forward. The wagon was painted with alternate splashes of red and blue, and two small American flags were fastened to it, one on each side opposite the driver.

"But he didn't stop there. Having adopted a patriotic red-white-and-blue motif for the day, it must have seemed only logical to him to go all the way: He had whitewashed his horse!

"We watched him, open-mouthed, until he passed out of our sight. Two or three hours later the gossip began to filter back to Goosetown. Honor, it seemed to say, is not always with the patriot.

"This day was, like so many San Jose Fourths of July, beastly hot, and by the time the ice cream man arrived uptown, the poor horse was sweating badly. That set the whitewash to running. It dribbled a trail along the street, and that led a pack of concerned citizens to conclude the horse was deathly ill or badly abused — or both.

"That's right: Somebody called the Humane Society, which in turn called the police. The poor ice cream man was hauled off to the pokey. Or that's the way we heard it anyway.

"I don't know to this day how the incident was resolved, just as I still don't know the ice cream man's name. But I know things must have worked out in the end because after a time there he was, selling ice cream cones off the back of his wagon again. We never asked him what happened; kids didn't do that in those days . . ."

January 7, 1981

It seems impossible to write about Goosetown without provoking a flurry of response from Goosetowners past and present.

Frank Bonanno, the *News* managing editor, popped in the other day to fuss at me about keeping the old name alive. Frank sees "Goose-

51

town" as something of an ethnic slur. "We've been trying to live that name down for years," says ex-Goosetowner Frank, "and you're not helping."

His complaint is tongue-in-cheek, of course. He knows it, and I know it, and he knows I know he knows it.

The fact, apparently, is that old Goosetowners never die; they just move to Willow Glen and write letters to the editor about the good old days and the good old folks in Goosetown.

THOUGH GOOSETOWN REMAINS LARGELY A STATE OF MIND, IT MAY BE HELPFUL TO FIT IT INTO SOME MODERN GEOGRAPHY. FOR EXAMPLE, THE CHILDREN'S DISCOVERY MUSEUM, ON THE WEST BANK OF THE GUADALUPE RIVER JUST SOUTH OF SAN CARLOS STREET, WOULD PROBABLY QUALIFY AS A GOOSETOWN RESIDENT, OR SOMETHING CLOSE TO IT. SO WOULD THE NEW MULTI-MILLION DOLLAR SAN JOSE CONVENTION CENTER FRONTING ON ALMADEN BOULEVARD (IT WAS UPGRADED FROM AVENUE AWHILE BACK) SOUTH OF SAN CARLOS STREET.

HARDBY OLD GOOSETOWN, THOUGH A TAD TO THE NORTH, ACROSS SAN CARLOS STREET, YOU WILL FIND THE CENTER FOR THE PERFORMING ARTS, THE CIVIC AUDITORIUM AND THE RIVER PARK TOWERS.

ULTIMATELY, THE TECHNOLOGY CENTER OF SILICON VALLEY WILL (IF ALL GOES AS PLANNED) JOIN THE CHILDREN'S DISCOVERY MUSEUM AS A GENUINE DENIZEN OF GOOSETOWN.

When Downtown Was Downtown it Had Community Spirit

March 12, 1980

IN 1980, WHEN DOWNTOWN REDEVEL-
OPMENT WAS A BITTER JOKE, I WROTE THAT
THE ROMANTIC (OR OPTIMIST) IN ME RE-
TAINED A CHILDLIKE FAITH THAT DOWN-
TOWN WOULD RISE AGAIN.

IF TALL BUILDINGS AND LUXURY HOTELS
A DOWNTOWN MAKE (AND THEY DO TO A
DEGREE) THEN THAT FAITH HAS BEEN REAL-
IZED LESS THAN A DECADE LATER.

IN RETROSPECT, MUCH OF WHAT I MUSED
OVER (AND PINED AFTER) HAS COME TO
PASS, AND MORE APPEARS TO BE IN REASON-
ABLE PROSPECT. BUT, TO LOOK BACK, HERE'S
HOW THINGS LOOKED TO ME ON MARCH
12, 1980.

Before 1956 downtown was *the* regional shopping center for the Santa Clara Valley. There were
neighborhood centers, to be sure: Lincoln Avenue
from Coe to Minnesota in Willow Glen, Santa
Clara's Franklin Street between the University of
Santa Clara and the Carmelite monastery, East
Santa Clara Street between 20th and 24th streets,
and what Eastsiders used to call Mayfair.

These had their unique character, but when
Mama and the girls said they were going "downtown," they meant downtown San Jose. (If, for
example, they were headed for Lincoln Avenue,
they'd probably say they were "going into Willow
Glen.")

Going downtown meant something substan-
tially different in the 1940s and 1950s than going
to Valley Fair or Eastridge means today. Now you
go to buy a raincoat or a dinner, and then you go
home again. When downtown was Downtown,
you couldn't separate your commercial from
your social life that easily.

Frankly I miss that. It started to slip away in
1956, when the first major store in Valley Fair, San
Jose's first regional shopping center, opened for
business.

Pre-1956 downtown had a lot going for it.
Geographically it was compact without being
cramped, extending as it did roughly from St.
James Park to San Salvador Street on its north-

south axis and between Market and Third streets, east-west.

Within this dozen square-block area San Joseans enjoyed four first-run movie houses, several smaller theaters, a clutch of restaurants ranging from continental to hole-in-the-wall-ethnic. All of the major department stores (Hart's, Hale's, Penney's, Blum's, Roos Bros.) were there, too, along with Montgomery Ward, Sears Roebuck, W. T. Grant and a full array of five-and-dimes (Kress's, Newberry's, Walgreen's.)

Then there were the specialty clothing shops (Prussia's was favored by ladies of taste and refinement) and stationers, photographers' studios, book stores, jewelers' shops, travel agencies, creameries, candy shops, furniture stores. You name it, downtown had it.

And it had two other indispensibles: people and accessibility.

Doctors, lawyers, bankers, barbers, beauticians, clerks, typists, cooks, waiters, gas station attendants, bowling alley pinboys, newspaper reporters — all of us worked downtown.

Because we were there, it made sense for the street cars, and later the buses, to converge on downtown. First and Santa Clara streets was, in literal fact, the crossroads of San Jose. Buses from Santa Clara, Willow Glen, Los Gatos, Evergreen and Alum Rock picked up and deposited passengers there. The sociological implications of this were enormous, and for the most part charming.

Because you and almost everybody you knew worked downtown, it was inevitable you'd meet a friend or acquaintance on your way to lunch. (And you didn't have to get in your car and drive for a half hour to find a decent place to eat.) Those noon-time sidewalk conversations slowed down foot traffic, but they speeded up the transmission of gossip, which in turn tended to promote a sense of community. (When you know what's going on, you know it's *your* town).

Because "everybody" had to go downtown for something at some time, Mama and the girls always dressed for the occasion. ("You never know who you're going to meet.") Dresses, hats, even gloves on holidays, were *de rigeur,* and girls who went downtown in shorts or pedal pushers were "common."

Youngsters of both sexes tended to be on their good behavior when downtown unchaperoned, whether they came on the bus for a dentist's appointment or biked in with the gang

South First Street, looking north from San Fernando Street, c. 1955. Del Carlo, photographer. San Jose Historical Museum collections.

for Coke and ice cream. They knew the odds were always excellent that any over-indulgence in high spirits would be noted and reported by some promenading adult friend of the family. ("You never know who you're going to meet.")

In retrospect, pre-1956 downtown was notable for what it didn't have, too. It didn't have adult bookstores, porno movie palaces, streetwalkers, winos and aggressive panhandlers. The occasional derelict who wandered up from the Southern Pacific freight yards generally didn't penetrate further than North Market Street. If he did, a beat cop escorted him back across that invisible but very real barrier.

I LIKED THE OLD DOWNTOWN, AND WHILE IT WON'T BE COMING BACK, WHAT BIDS FAIR TO TAKE ITS PLACE IS MORE THAN WELCOME. THE NEW DOWNTOWN PROMISES TO BE DYNAMIC AND EXCITING. IT'S BOUND TO BE BIGGER (VERTICALLY AS WELL AS HORIZONTALLY); WITH ANY LUCK IT WILL BE BETTER AS WELL.

South First Street, 1944. Stelling, photographer. San Jose Historical Museum collections.

"Making Do" in a Housing Shortage

May 7, 1980

Anybody who thinks the jobs-housing imbalance is a new phenomenon here is either a Johnny-come-lately or afflicted with a Swiss cheese memory.

The point isn't that there's a problem; the point is how you cope.

Over the years, San Joseans have experienced periodic housing shortages, and they have coped in different ways; though in general, the efforts shake down into two categories: Bug Out or Make Do.

The second California Legislature took the first route in 1851.

The first Legislature convened here in 1849, a full year before California was admitted to the Union, and, finding the accommodations less than sumptuous, proceeded to dull the pain with bargain basement whiskey. That became the legendary "Legislature of a Thousand Drinks."

The second Legislature assembled in February, 1851, found San Jose still lacking in five-star boarding houses, and in May moved the capital of California from San Jose to Vallejo. Neither the capital nor the Legislature ever came back, which must be counted a mixed blessing.

My own confrontation of the jobs-housing crisis is of more recent vintage.

In 1946, the United States Army returned me from a walking tour of Europe and, at the separation center in Ft. Dix, New Jersey, bade me a heartfelt "get lost." Whereupon, I headed home to San Jose with the uniform on my back, a fistful of travel pay and the first $100 installment of the World War II enlisted man's $300 mustering-out bonus. (The Veterans Administration mailed you the other $200, at the rate of $100 a month, once you established a civilian residence. That way, you couldn't drink it up all at once.)

It was the mustering-out pay that enabled me to Make Do in San Jose's post-war jobs-housing brouhaha.

In 1946, San Jose had not yet begun to experience the growing pains that would make it the fourth largest city in California. Our town was still largely the food-processing county seat we had left at the beginning of the war; single-family

Airport Village, 1949, provided temporary housing for veterans and their families on the grounds of the San Jose Municipal Airport. Mercury News photo.

homes were the rule, apartments the exception.

Also, during the war nobody built homes or apartments; guns, tanks and planes had priority. Consequently, when a flood of newly minted civilians descended on the town (and on San Jose State College and the University of Santa Clara), what few pre-war apartments there were went to the swift and the cunning. That left me out on two counts.

How to Make Do?

An old friend and former teacher, Carl W. Palmer, provided the answer in an unexpected way. In the course of renewing old acquaintances, I had dropped in on the Palmers in their Palm-haven district home.

"Where will you be staying?" Carl asked.

"Beats me," I answered. "You looking for a boarder?"

He wasn't and the conversation languished. Then he brightened. "Say," he said, "I've got an idea." It turned out to be the Make Do idea.

Carl wanted to build a guest cottage at the rear of his garage, but he didn't have the money. I had money (that $300 mustering-out pay), but

no place to build a guest cottage. I had no skills with which to build one, either, but Carl said not to worry. I'd buy the materials, we'd build the place together, and I could live in it rent-free for as long as I wanted, or until I finished college.

And that's the way it happened. Carl was a passable do-it-yourself carpenter and had, in addition, spent the early war years as a shipyard electrician. And — miracle of miracles — his neighbor, Bruce McDonald, was a plumbing contractor.

Carl and Bruce provided the technical know-how, and I provided the money and unskilled labor. We made an unbeatable team.

The upshot of it all is that I lived undisturbed and undismayed by San Jose's post-World War II jobs-housing imbalance, at the rear of Hartford Avenue until well into my senior year in college. In fact, I didn't give the place up until I was preparing to return to Paris for postgraduate study.

No big deal. I was just Making Do — with the help of some friendly San Joseans. There are still a lot of them around. It's that kind of town.

Quest Club Members Get Together to Eat, Drink and Think

July 2, 1980

To adapt a description from Damon Runyon, Quest Club is San Jose's oldest permanently established floating intellectual crap game. It's worth passing mention for a couple of reasons.

First, any organization that can survive 64 years without a constitution, officers, rules, dues or a messianic mission is noteworthy in itself.

Second, in an era of feminism and affirmative action, Quest Club is a paradox. It manages to be good-humoredly undemocratic, elitist, sexist and civilizing all at the same time. It is part of what makes San Jose unique.

Quest Club was founded in the spring of 1916 by three wildly individualistic lawyers who drifted into San Jose shortly after the turn of the century. One, Grant R. Bennett, had organized a troop of Texas cavalry and hiked up San Juan Hill with Teddy Roosevelt. In San Jose he practiced labor law, which in those days was another uphill walk.

The second, Paul Fenimore Clark, spurred the citizens of Willow Glen to incorporate, and then became their first mayor, in order to fight the Southern Pacific railroad. The SP wanted to relocate its mainline tracks through Clark's neighborhood, and he was having none of it.

The third, Charles Sumner Allen Sr., was a Nebraska corporation lawyer who came West for his health, settling in San Jose. He taught international law at the College of the Pacific before it moved to Stockton, was for a decade chief editorial writer of the old *Mercury Herald* and served 24 years as a member of the San Jose Board of Education.

When this unlikely trio founded Quest Club they weren't looking for notoriety; each of them had achieved enough of that already. They were looking for good fellowship, good spirits and the chance to sharpen their wits on one another in the name of good citizenship. They succeeded so remarkably their spiritual descendants are still at it.

From 1916 unto today, club members have gathered in each other's homes twice a month, summers excluded, to exchange views (and occasional recriminations) on the news of the the

This undated photo captures the San Jose Quest Club's three founders: Rough Rider Grant R. Bennett is seated at far right, hat in lap. Law professor-editorial writer Charley Allen is the man sporting a staw boater. Paul Fenimore Clark, Willow Glen's first mayor, peeks between the two men at far left.

day, to eat and drink and — most importantly — to listen to, dissect and evaluate the host member's research paper.

Over the years, the club's membership has been weighted heavily toward college professors, doctors, lawyers, architects, ranchers, industrialists, business executives and just enough newspapermen to ensure a note of commonality.

Quest Club isn't unique in concept, of course. Other communities have its counterpart, the conscious model for which is the Literary Club of Dr. Samuel Johnson. Through it, the essayist-lexicographer was instrumental in shaping the tastes and manners of 18th century London.

Nobody pretends Quest Club is or ever was in that league, but it has set and maintained a respectable level of discourse. The club's roster over the years suggests why.

At one time or another, Quest Club members included: Dr. Tully Knowles, president of College of the Pacific; Dr. Thomas W. MacQuarrie, who guided San Jose State College from just after World War I into the 1950s; George L. Sullivan, dean of the University of Santa Clara School of Engineering and the man who master-planned modern San Jose's sewage-collection system; Superior Court Judge William F. James, after whom Santa Clara County's boys' ranch is named; Dr. Dwight Bissell, for years San Jose city health officer; Pierce Davies, one-time managing editor of the *Mercury*

Herald and later a professor of journalism at San Jose State. The list isn't inclusive, only representative.

Quest Club prides itself on having no rules. Tradition governs, the longest-held tradition being that membership is by invitation only, and only men get invited.

That may have been fine in 1916, but its days as an operating principle may be numbered. Last year the club was shaken by Ruth's Revolt.

Ruth is Ruth Smith, a talented, feisty woman who is the wife of club member Olney Smith, director of planning for the City of Santa Clara. Why, Ruth wanted to know, are women permitted only to serve refreshments and attend the annual season's-end barbecue in June? Why, she persisted, can't women present research papers, too?

The men scratched their heads and said they couldn't think of any reason, really. Except tradition. Caught with their rationalization down, they penciled Ruth in for a paper this year.

She didn't give one; it was the principle of the thing, she explained. But don't bet she won't present a research paper someday, complete with the requisite charts, graphs and other visual aids. That's how traditions are born.

FOUR YEARS AFTER THIS THUMBNAIL HISTORY OF THE QUEST CLUB APPEARED IN THE SAN JOSE MERCURY NEWS, THE CLUB EXPIRED.

Bob Doerr Gets People's Attention and Gets Things Done

September 10-17, 1980

Some people are memorable. You see them once, you never forget them. Robert C. Doerr is memorable.

In the past 40 years I've seen Bob Doerr countless times. It would have been hard not to — he's been a San Jose city councilman, mayor, redevelopment board member and county grand juror— but I still remember the first time I laid eyes on him. It was in a ninth-grade social studies classroom in Herbert Hoover Junior High School.

I was a less than enthusiastic scholar, Bob a substitute teacher. Ordinarily, that's not a promising combination. Bob proved to be extraordinary.

He bounced into the classroom, smoothed back a mop of wavy blond hair with one hand and drew himself up to his full height.

"Today," he intoned, "we're going to learn about American history." Groans from the class. "Starting with baseball." End of groans, beginning of attention span.

Whereupon he launched into the finest dramatic interpretation of "Casey at the Bat," complete with gestures, it has ever been my privilege to witness. Here, we concluded, was a man worth listening to; we kept on listening avidly long after Casey and the Mudville Nine gave way to James Monroe and his Doctrine.

"It was an old trick," Bob conceded with a grin years later, "but a useful one. And not really dirty. You've got to get people's attention before you can accomplish anything."

We Hoover ninth-graders couldn't know that Bob Doerr would go places and accomplish much. In fact, we didn't even know where he came from, which was San Jose, or that his family was one of the first to settle in the Santa Clara Valley. Had we known, we probably wouldn't have cared; generational sagas are lost on the young.

Still, it's worth noting that Bob's grandfather, Charles Doerr, emigrated from Germany in 1858, primarily to escape service in the Prussian army. Here he joined a brother, Phillip, who had come in 1853 for the same reason and who established the New York Bakery on the site of today's retail Pavillion.

Charles went to work in the bakery, and eventually bought it from Phillip at 170 South First Street, where Fred Doerr, Bob's father, was born in 1875 — upstairs, over the ovens.

But the Doerrs didn't live by bread alone. Phillip went on to found the San Jose Brewery, at Fourth and William streets, an enterprise that, alas, didn't stay in the family.

"We were never quite clear how Great Uncle Phillip got out of the brewing business," Bob sighs, "but the rest of us always considered it something of a tragedy."

Perhaps to console themselves, the Doerrs took to politics. Charles served a six-year term on the San Jose City Council in the late 1890s; Fred was a councilman from 1924 until 1942, serving two years as president of the council — the equivalent of mayor. Bob served three non-consecutive terms on the council, 1950-54 and 1956-64; he was mayor in 1956-58.

It was Bob Doerr who, as mayor, sold the city council on the need for a thorough-going examination of human relations in San Jose. By then, he had the council's attention.

"My first term I spent being the brash young man with liberal ideas," Bob explains. "Later I learned you can get a lot more done if you listen a little as well as talk."

Anyway, Doerr's study committee led to the creation of San Jose's first Human Relations Committee, the forerunner of today's county-wide body.

Doerr also was instrumental in plunging San Jose into the international sister cities program, through which we now maintain cultural and civic ties with Okayama, Japan; San Jose, Costa Rica; Tainan, Taiwan; and Veracruz, Mexico. For years he headed the international relations section of the American Municipal Association, the forerunner of the National League of Cities.

Bob Doerr's interest in world affairs is no accident. While still a student at San Jose State College, he spent summers traveling in Europe, principally Germany, and he became by turns fascinated and appalled by Adolph Hitler. It was a study Bob was to pursue for the next 40 years as a teacher and politician.

When World War II burst on America, the Army took one look at Bob's educational background and his fluency in German and bundled him into the Counter-Intelligence Corps. And it was as a CIC agent that Bob found himself in bombed-out Berlin in the days immediately after *Gotterdammerung.* His mission: find out what really happened to Hitler. Bob and his unit established beyond reasonable doubt that Adolf Hitler did, in fact, blow his brains out in the *Fuhrerbunker* as the Red Army pounded the Reichstag chancellery to rubble over his head.

"Everyone said I should have written a book about that experience," Bob recalls with a sigh, "but I was in the Army, and you know how that goes."

H. R. Trevor-Roper, the British historian, wasn't in the U.S. Army, and his *The Last Days of Hitler* has become a classic. One more item for the That's Life Department.

Later, in 1965 to be exact, the city of Munich commissioned Bob to research and publish a disinterested history of that city's anti-Nazi underground. "Munich: Culprit or Scapegoat" was the result. He used a sabbatical year from teaching in San Jose to produce it.

During 12 years on the city council, Bob Doerr became San Jose's expert on urban affairs abroad. As head of the American Municipal Association's international relations section, he spent summers watching local officials in Western Europe and Asia grappling with their problems.

"The remarkable thing," Bob says, "is that the problems are pretty much the same here as there — traffic, waste disposal, pollution, transit, land use planning. Only the people and their approaches to the problems are different.

"Take annexations, for instance. Here the people can pretty much decide which city, if any, they'll join or whether they'll form their own city — as they did in Campbell, Milpitas and Saratoga in recent years in order to avoid being absorbed into San Jose. In West Germany they would have been spared the agony of decision; the state would have made it for them. When post-war Munich was pushing outward, much like San Jose, the Bavarian state government merely pulled

Mayor and Mrs. Robert C. Doerr being welcomed by Kenzo Sato, chief of the Tokyo office of Okayama Prefecture, upon their arrival in Japan during the first anniversary celebration of the San Jose-Okayama sister-city affiliation. May 1958.

up the city limits signs and put them down again just ahead of the expanding population.

"The prevailing philosophy in Europe is that it doesn't matter who provides municipal service; it's only important that the people be served. I'm not sure we're ready for that here yet."

Still, Bob is persuaded that some form of metropolitan government must come ultimately to the Bay Area.

"We probably should tear up all the city and county boundaries and start over on a functional, rather than a geographical, basis." For example, he grinned, warming to the subject "we might elect a series of councils, each with a different set of responsibilities. The largest would be region-wide and would handle clearly regional functions — smog control, sewerage, transportation,

land use planning, as opposed to precise zoning. That sort of thing.

"Next we might step down to a metropolitan council, which would provide specific services, such as police and fire protection, garbage disposal and libraries, to the metropolises — San Jose, Oakland and San Francisco.

"For those who attach great sentimental value to historic place names and/or who do most of their living in their immediate neighborhoods, we could have a third, and perhaps even a fourth level of 'local' government. City and neighborhood councils would decide such matters as the kind of fence appropriate in a residential neighborhood or the precise location of a factory within an established industrial zone.

"We Americans are supposed to be the world's

62

greatest inventors. We need a political invention about now to deal with urban growth because it's not slackening."

As far as San Jose is concerned, Bob doesn't see the new 10-district council as a new political invention.

"For the first 65 years of our corporate history," Bob recalls, "we had council districts — we called them wards. My grandfather was elected from the old Third Ward. Then in 1915, San Joseans adopted a city charter that gave us a seven-member council elected at large. My father and I served under that system. I don't see either one as inherently superior to the other. Everything goes back to the quality of men and women who serve."

BOB DOERR LIVES IN RETIREMENT IN SAN JOSE. HE STILL ENJOYS TRAVELLING AND PARTICIPATING IN COMMUNITY AFFAIRS.

Hayes Mansion Has Historical Past, Condominiums in Its Future

October 15, 1980

Mary Folsom Hayes-Chynoweth was born in upstate New York in 1825, the daughter of a Free Will Baptist preacher and the ninth of 10 children. She grew up poor, but she died rich — in 1905 in the South San Jose mansion that bears her name and whose future now sparks heated municipal controversy.

In her 80 years, Mary Hayes-Chynoweth was a teacher, a spiritual healer, founder and principal sermonizer of The True Life Church, and a believer, far ahead of her time, in the efficacy of health foods. She was also a canny business-woman who believed in thrift, solid construction and Doing Right.

In all probability, Mary Hayes-Chynoweth would be firmly in the corner of those, including Dorothy Silva, Lilyann Brannon and Velma Lisher, who want the people of San Jose to create the Edenvale Historical Landmark District in order to preserve the Hayes mansion and the 50-odd acres of adjoining trees that for 19 years sheltered Frontier Village amusement park. Mary built her

Mary Hayes Chynoweth. San Jose Historical Museum collections.

house and planned its grounds for an extended future.

Now, the condominiums threaten to march deeper into Edenvale. Rio Grande Industries,

Hayes mansion in its heyday. San Jose Historical Museum collections.

which owns the Frontier Village property, is dickering with developers. Dr. Stanley Lourdeaux, the Los Altos proctologist who has owned the Hayes mansion off and on for 22 years, is looking for a buyer again.

Thus the struggle is joined. Silva-Brannon-Lisher *et al* have nothing against condominiums; they just don't want them *instead* of a 62-room structure that has been on the National Historic Register since 1975. They wouldn't mind saving the Frontier Village trees, either; the big ones date from the late 1880s when the widow Mary Hayes and her sons, Everis Anson and Jay Orley, were farming the 240 acres and planning the mansion.

For the Hayes clan of that era, money was no object. The Hayeses were respectable Wisconsin farmers (Mary's first husband, Anson E. Hayes was a cousin of President Rutherford B. Hayes) who struck it rich through Mary's effort. She credited divine inspiration for leading her to a series of rich iron deposits in Wisconsin and Michigan. The family developed them and prospered.

Consequently, by 1887, when the 240-acre estate to be called Eden Vale began to take shape, the Hayes family was well placed to become part

of the early San Jose Establishment. E.A. and J.O. (called Red and Black respectively for the color of their beards) were university graduates, practicing attorneys and businessmen-farmers. They would go on to politics and newspaper publishing as well.

During this period, Mary Hayes was busy founding The True Life Church, overseeing family enterprises and planning the first Hayes mansion. (In 1890 she remarried, but her second husband, T.B. Chynoweth, a family friend from Wisconsin, died a scant 10 months after the wedding.)

The first Hayes mansion to go up in Edenvale, a four-story wood-frame Victorian structure, burned to the ground in 1899. The trauma impacted heavily on Mary Hayes-Chynoweth — and on E.A. and J.O. Hayes; they had just reduced the insurance coverage on the building from $100,000 to $75,000. Determined not to be burned out a second time, Mary hired a San Jose architect, George W. Page, and told him, apparently, to build a structure capable of withstanding anything. Page complied.

Construction went forward from 1899 to 1905 on the three-story Mediterranean-style villa that still stands today. Its structural brick walls are 19

Interior of the Hayes Mansion library. San Jose Historical Museum collections.

inches thick, and the interior is finished in three-quarter-inch plaster and stucco over expanded metal lath. Brass doors separate three of the wings, and the fourth, which contains the kitchen, is virtually free standing, being separated from the rest of the house by a conservatory. Internal fire-fighting stations are located on each floor, and auxiliary water tanks were located on the third floor. In addition, the basement under each wing (the structure is built in the shape of a Maltese cross) is self-contained; fire in one can't spread to another and thus endanger the whole structure.

That's probably why the Hayes mansion survived California's killer earthquake of 1906 with little more than cracked plaster. It's why arsonists, scavengers and the just-plain-careless have been able to vandalize its beauty but only chip away at its structural soundness.

Many of the marble fireplace facings, the hand-crafted terazzo tiles and the damask wall coverings have been looted, but the remarkable woodwork of the mansion remains. Fourteen varieties of hard and soft woods were utilized in finishing the interior suites, which, even in ruins, tend to make the Winchester Mystery House look tacky by comparison.

Is the Hayes mansion worth saving, on architectural and/or historical grounds? The answer has to be: Sure, if the price is right. It will, in fact, cost a bundle either to restore or demolish the Hayes mansion; it's that sturdy.

As an example of 19th century Mediterranean-villa architecture, the mansion may well be unique. In terms of local history, the building is undeniably one of a kind.

The Hayes family played a key role in building San Jose and the Santa Clara Valley. "Red" Hayes served seven terms in the House of Representatives (1904-1918), where he helped write the Federal Reserve Act and delivered his maiden speech in 1905, against Japanese immigration. (A measure of changing times: "Red" Hayes' seat is now filled by Representative Norman Y. Mineta, a Nisei.)

"Black" Hayes helped organize the California Prune and Apricot Growers Association (now called Sunsweet Growers) and ran unsuccessfully for governor of California in 1918.

Together, the brothers, both staunch Republicans, formed the Good Government League to fight corruption in San Jose City Hall. In the course of this endeavor, they bought the *San Jose Herald* in 1900 and, a year later, acquired controlling interest in the *San Jose Mercury*. The *Mercury-Herald,* and later the *San Jose Evening News* as well, continued in Hayes family ownership until 1952, when they were sold. Two years later, the family sold the Edenvale mansion, too.

The newspapers survive, as part of the Knight-Ridder publishing group. The Hayes mansion survives also — but barely. What happens to it now is up to the people of San Jose.

IN 1985 THE CITY OF SAN JOSE PURCHASED THE HAYES ESTATE BECAUSE OF ITS EXTRAORDINARY BEAUTY AND IMPORTANCE TO THE CITY'S HISTORY. FUTURE PLANS MAY INCLUDE BOTH RESTORATION AND ADAPTIVE REUSE OF THE STRUCTURE FOR EITHER A CIVIC OR COMMERCIAL PURPOSE.

Dwight Bissell
A Sense of Humor and a Sense of Health

November 5, 1980

Dwight M. Bissell went to work for the City of San Jose on January 1, 1942; on January 2, he underwent an unsettling but useful introduction to the life of a city health officer.

"Bill Champion (then a city sanitarian) took me over to North First Street and into a butcher shop," Dr. Bissell recalled with a wry grin last week. "Right up front was a blood-stained chopping block, and right on top of the block was a sticky-furred cat. Sound asleep. There was a lot of that going around back then."

There was a certain amount of botulism going around, too, attributable to the home-canned cactus some North Market Street restaurants favored as a chile spice. There were open privies in the town's northeast quadrant because the sanitary sewer system didn't extend out there. And there were periodic infestations of mosquitos that threatened, though they rarely produced, outbreaks of dengue and yellow fever.

Even by the relatively casual standards of that day, San Jose was a challenging place to practice public health.

Dwight M. Bissell, M.D., 1945. Mercury News photo.

And Dwight Montgomery Bissell, a Fresno farm boy turned school teacher turned doctor turned public health officer, couldn't resist the challenge. Today, at age 77 and formally retired, he still can't let one go by.

The son of a Fresno peach and raisin farmer, Dwight worked his way through Fresno State College, becoming a public school teacher to earn enough money to go to medical school. The process took 11 years, half of them falling within the time frame of the Great Depression. (Dwight Bissell received his M.D. degree from Stanford University in 1936. He also holds a master's degree in education from Stanford and a master's degree in public health from the University of California, Berkeley.)

Two days a week, he supervises the nursing care for patients as a director of the Santa Clara County Council on Aging, he has been instrumental in setting up nutrition programs that serve hot, balanced meals to oldsters in a dozen locations. "It's as much for the socialization as for the food," he says. "Getting old is hard; getting old in isolation is too hard."

And he is grass-roots politicking in the cause of adult day health care. Why not, he argues, set up day care centers for the ambulatory elderly, men and women who aren't yet ready for a rest home but who still need somebody to look after them while the family is at work or school?

Why not? It's a good question, and it typifies Dwight Bissell's approach to problems in general and public health in particular. Official San Jose became intimately familiar with Dwight Bissel's "Why not" from 1942 through 1965. Those were the years during which he ran the city with restless energy, political deftness and an impish sense of humor that he learned ultimately to control, but only imperfectly and with great difficulty.

An early and memorable lesson in humor control was administered by Clyde Fischer, then a member of the city council.

"As health officer, I had to attend council meetings," Dwight said grinning. "You know, to answer questions from the councilmen and all. Well one night after the regular meeting, Clyde

came up to me and asked, 'Doctor, what's causing these bald spots?' He pushed back his hair —he was wearing it long then — and pointed to a couple patches of skin. I took a look and said, 'Why, Mr. Councilman, I know of only one thing that can cause that: syphilis!' "

Clyde, who is a mortician by trade and a pillar of rectitude by temperament, did not suffer from syphilis or any other social disease. He was not amused, and he never voted for another health department appropriation during his term on the council. And he frequently raised questions concerning the propriety of the city health officer's serving as San Jose School District physician and lecturing at San Jose State College (in public health) and at Stanford Medical School.

Not all hale fellows are well met; it's the kind of political lesson learned best on the job. In general, Dwight Bissell absorbed it well enough. His wit did not, for example, preclude him from playing a major role in founding the Visiting Nurses Association; and it may have helped him jolly fellow physicians in the County Medical

Old City of San Jose Health Department office in City Plaza. San Jose Historical Museum collections.

Society into staffing a series of ongoing disease control and blindness prevention programs.

It didn't hurt, apparently, when he lobbied San Jose voters successfully on behalf of sewer construction bond elections and when he set up regular immunization and well-baby clinics and initiated the city's first training program for food handlers.

Nor did it stop him from organizing one of San Jose's first mental health clinics for children and adults and from setting up the community's first half-way house for the rehabilitation of patients released from Agnews State Hospital.

Bet a sense of humor was no help at all in cleaning out San Jose's mosquito menace. Dwight and the city health department managed that by breeding and distributing Gambusia affinis, a tiny trash fish that thrives on mosquito larvae. The problem is, Gambusia have a passion for goldfish eggs, too. San Joseans who topped off their fish-ponds with health department Gambusia got rid of their mosquitos and, after a time, their gold-fish, too. Fish lovers who were counting on natural increases to keep their ponds stocked were, like Clyde Fischer before them, not amused. Still, the program worked, which from the standpoint of eradicating mosquito-borne diseases, was the main thing.

DWIGHT BISSELL LIVED IN QUIET RETIRE-MENT IN SARATOGA FOR MANY YEARS AND DIED IN APRIL 1989.

Dr. Dwight Bissell, Councilman Robert Welch, Councilman Joseph Pace, and City Manager Dutch Hamann at the groundbreaking of the addition to the Health Department. San Jose Historical Museum collections.

Doctor Worked to Defeat Disease
That Almost Defeated Him

November 26, 1980

By Carl F. Heintze

To some, it was the White Scourge; to others, it was the White Death. By whatever name it was known, it spelled terror.

Brought to the United States in the 1840s by immigrants fleeing the potato famines of Ireland, it spread across American towns and cities — crippling, killing, incapacitating. Neither rich nor poor, neither young nor old were spared. It came to mark millions.

It was tuberculosis, TB, a disease now so seldom seen in this country that most Americans have forgotten it exists. But it was very much a part of Santa Clara County in 1948, when a young internist just out of Stanford Medical School arrived at Santa Clara County Hospital, now Valley Medical Center.

He was R. Morton Manson, who at the end of 1980 steps down as its director of medical education and assistant director of county medical institutions.

"The three great accomplishments of medicine I've seen in my lifetime are the almost complete eradication in this country of smallpox, poliomyelitis and tuberculosis," Mort Manson says.

Of these three killers, Dr. Manson's principal enemy has been tuberculosis — and for good reason. Before he finished medical school, he had contracted the disease. In the first half of this century, this wasn't unusual. Many physicians were stricken with TB while caring for its victims. Sometimes both doctor and patient died.

Mort Manson's case, while severe, eventually was overcome, but it also gave him a special reason to want to wipe out TB. In 1948, this didn't seem all that possible. A considerable amount was understood about how the TB bacillus found its way into the body and what it did after it arrived. But not much was known about how to combat it once it infected human beings.

Usually TB began in the lungs. It was carried by aerosols, minute particles of water, coughed out into the atmosphere by its victims and inhaled by others. But it could affect any other part of the body. If it reached the meninges, the lining of the brain, it could kill quickly.

Treatment in the early 1940s consisted mostly of isolation of the patient . . . to prevent him from spraying others with the germ . . . lots of rest, fresh air and sunshine. Both the isolation and the rest might last a long time.

Some believed that forcing the lung into a more compact shape might help prevent the disease from spreading. To foster this, air was pumped into the cavity around the lung, a procedure which had to be repeated every couple of weeks.

When Dr. Manson arrived at VMC, the hospital had a 144-bed TB isolation ward where 200 such procedures were carried out every week. TB was big business. In fact, it was a good part of VMC's total treatment package in those days.

With this in mind, hospital officials applied to the federal government to build what is now called the "seven-story building" at VMC. Its upper four floors were to be a tuberculosis sanatorium to house the patients then occupying the old sanatorium built in the 1920s. These lay beyond the main hospital.

But even as the funds were being approved and construction was begun, the control of TB was under way. The story was bound up in chemotherapy, the use of drugs.

First streptomycin was licensed for use. It was followed by a second drug called PAS. Later PAS and streptomycin were used in combination.

Then in the 1950s, isoniazid and rifampin, both highly effective drugs with no severe side effects, came into the market. The four floors which were to have been set aside for TB patients at VMC shrank to two, then to one.

For a time in the 1950s and 1960s, it remained as an isolation area for TB inpatients, a kind of island shut off from the rest of the hospital. Its population, never very large, was usually bored and isolated from the rest of the world.

Although educational programs were set up by the Campbell School District and rehabilitation was undertaken by the State Department of Rehabilitation, TB patients still were shut away from others.

R. Morton Manson, M.D. Photo courtesy of Mrs. R. Morton Manson.

Then, in the early 1970s TB experts concluded that the disease is of low potential infection without almost direct contact between patients and others. Even the seventh floor isolation was no longer needed. Besides, the number of patients was so low that it was not economically justifiable to keep the separate floor open.

Today, TB patients, whenever they do appear, are cared for in individual isolation rooms at VMC for a short time and then put out on regular floors.

Many weeks now pass at VMC without the appearance of a single TB infection.

Little else remains of the TB era either. The old Chest Clinic managed by Dr. Robert Rowan after Dr. Manson moved up to his present job in 1959 was torn down last year to make way for a new inpatient psychiatric building. The Institute for Medical Research building replaced the last old sanatorium that once opened its windows to sunshine and light, then the only cures for the disease.

And now Mort Manson himself is leaving the hospital. In many ways, it seems the end of an era. Known to literally hundreds of Santa Clara County physicians and VMC employees, Dr. Manson in many ways is VMC. He has been the "interim pope" for successive administrations, serving during four changes of director.

All that, however, isn't as important to Mort Manson, perhaps, as the final defeat of the enemy that almost defeated him at a time now long past in the battle against disease.

AFTER HIS FINAL STINT AS DIRECTOR OF VALLEY MEDICAL CENTER, MORT MANSON SERVED AS MEDICAL DIRECTOR OF LOCKHEED MISSILES AND SPACE CO., SUNNYVALE, UNTIL HIS DEATH IN MARCH, 1988.

Clark Bradley's Roots Have Served Him Well

February 25, 1981

I figure when a man has practiced law for 50 years from the same building in the same town, his neighbors are entitled to know a little bit more about him than you normally find in *Who's Who.*

For that matter, Clark Bradley isn't in *Who's Who,* though I suspect he ought to be.

Clark will be 73 this June 18, and he's still practicing law on a limited basis, "tapering off on probate matters now" is how he describes it. He practices as he always has, alone, and his office on the sixth floor of the Bank of the West building at First and Santa Clara streets isn't much different from the seventh-floor one he moved into in November, 1931, fresh out of Hastings College of Law in San Francisco.

Clark's record of public service is notable — eight years on the San Jose City Council, including a stint as mayor, nine years in the Assembly, 11 years in the state Senate. He laid the groundwork for ridding San Jose of machine politics; he helped defeat a proposed municipal takeover of the San Jose Water Works. He authored the basic state law that cut cities and counties in on the sales tax bonanza, and in his years in Sacramento, he earned the title of the "most conservative" member of the Legislature. Clark still enjoys the accolade.

That's the public Clark L. Bradley, or some small portion of him. Is there a different private Clark Bradley? Not really, though the essential individual is considerably more interesting than the "most conservative" label might suggest.

The United States was mired in what it called the Great War when, in the summer of 1918, a 10-year-old Clark Bradley arrived in San Jose with his newly divorced mother, Mae Clark Bradley. The two of them moved in temporarily with Mrs. Bradley's parents at 696 S. Fifth Street (a location now under the 280 Freeway). The elder Clarks had discovered San Jose during a tour of the West at the turn of the century and, entranced with what they saw, sold their farm near Climax, Michigan to settle here.

In short order, Mrs. Bradley and Clark established themseves at 54 S. Eighth Street and the slight, blond youngster enrolled in Lowell Grammar School. In temperament and attitude, he brought his Midwest heritage of thrift, diligence and application with him.

Clark Bradley was born June 18, 1908, in Topeka, Kansas, the only child of Mae and Glenn Bradley. "Somehow or other," Clark recalls, "my mother and father got involved in running a refrigeration plant in Topeka, and that's how I happened to be born there, but the plant went bust, and we moved back to Michigan. My earliest recollections are of Ann Arbor, where my father was studying for his doctorate in history at the University of Michigan." (The elder Bradley eventually came to head the history department at the University of Toledo).

There were other memories, too, of the small general store in Climax, down by the Indiana border, run by the Clarks who had stayed behind, and of the Bradley farm near Coldwater, in Branch County, 160 acres awarded to great-grandfather Howard Bradley in 1839 by the government of the United States.

"I've still got the grant deed here somewhere," Clark said, smiling proudly, as he turned to his office safe and fiddled with the combination. "Yep, here it is." He dusted off a large, yellowing envelope and extracted the folded parchment. Dated May 1, 1839, and signed by President Martin Van Buren, it conveyed the first 40 acres of a 160-acre section of public land to one Howard Bradley, farmer. The other three quarter-sections were added to the Bradley family holdings in subsequent years.

"I still own the farm," Clark said, with no little satisfaction. "It's never been out of the family."

And until Clark and his mother moved West, the Bradleys were never long out of Michigan. Glenn Bradley's brief bout with the Topeka refrigeration plant was something of a family aberration, Clark says.

Historically, the Bradleys were midwesterners who believed in, and lived, the work ethic. They conserved and improved what they had, whether it was land or an agile mind. They believed that free citizens owed something to their communities as well as to themselves, and they passed

Clark Bradley, 1974. Mercury News photo.

this heritage down from one generation to another. They were not, in the Midwestern idiom, flighty. It is a point of pride with Clark that his father, grandfather and great-grandfather lie buried side by side in the cemetery at Coldwater, Michigan.

Thus it was not surprising that Clark L. Bradley, displaced Midwesterner, approached life in San Jose with the same set of values. He worked hard, in school and out, and because fortune had removed him from the land, he concentrated on cultivating his agile mind. He managed the debate teams both at San Jose High School and San Jose State College and won a number of debate medals on his own. In his spare time, he attended San Jose City Council meetings and drafted the constitution for the Associated Students of San Jose State.

"Half way through State," Clark recalls, "I learned that Hastings would accept you if you had the equivalent of a junior college diploma, 60 credits. So I applied, and they accepted me. I was the second youngest member of my law school class."

Mayor Clark Bradley presiding over a meeting of the San Jose City Council. Left to right: George Starbird, Robert C. Doerr, Fred Watson, R. Cassin, Dorothy Covill, Mayor Clark Bradley, City Manager Dutch Hamann, Al Ruffo, Parker Hathaway, and Vic Owens. August 1951. San Jose Historical Museum collections.

He may well have been the most dedicated, too. Every day for three years he commuted round trip to San Francisco to read law, and he passed the bar on the first try. Every member of that Hastings class of 1931 passed the state bar examination, a feat few law schools can boast of today.

Once he set up a law practice here and began to ease his way into politics, it was inevitable that the private Clark Bradley should slide into the shadow of the public man, but they've never been disparate personalities. Democratic majorities repeatedly returned Clark, a conservative Republican, to Sacramento precisely because he lived those Midwestern values. He always said what he meant, meant what he said, read every bill he ever voted on and treated the opposition with courtesy and humor.

Come to think of it, a man like that doesn't need to be in *Who's Who*. He's known where it counts — among his friends and neighbors.

February 18, 1981

Clark L. Bradley, the former San Jose mayor, assemblyman and state senator, got to musing the other day about how he became, almost by accident, the father of the San Jose Unified School District.

That happened 41 years ago this spring, when San Jose voters approved four of five City Charter amendments sponsored by then-city councilman Bradley. All five were aimed at smashing the political machine of ambulance operator and liquor distributor Charlie Bigley, and, as Bradley recalls, the school issue was something less than central to his plans.

"Charlie never messed with the schools." Bradley said, smiling, "and I don't suppose he ever would have (Bigley's love of children was legendary in depression-era San Jose), but he could have. That was the problem."

Bigley controlled the city council by managing always to keep four of its seven members beholden to him for election or re-election. The council hired the city manager, who hired, among others, the superintendent of schools. The superintendent appointed the five-member school board, with council approval.

Bradley was right, of course. Charlie Bigley could have run the schools if he'd wanted to, but that wasn't Charlie's style. Instead, he told City Manager Clarence Goodwin whom to hire and whom to promote in the police and fire departments, and Goodwin, who owed his job to Bigley's city council majority, listened.

"All that bothered me," Bradley reflected.

"I was always interested in politics and government and I used to attend city council meetings Monday nights, even while I was still in high school. That's where I learned about Clarence Goodwin and Charlie Bigley, and it bothered me. Clarence was basically an honest man, but he was pliable."

Bradley determined either to stiffen Clarence Goodwin's backbone or get rid of him, but the high school civics student had a far piece to travel first. After he graduated from San Jose High School in 1926, Bradley attended San Jose State College for two years and transferred to the University of California's Hastings College of Law in San Francisco. Bradley earned his law degree in May 1931 and opened an office in the old First National Bank building that November.

He set about building a practice, got married in 1933 and, by 1936, decided he was ready to take on the Bigley-Goodwin machine. He was wrong. Bradley ran for a seat on the council that year and finished ninth in a field of 10. Two years later, he ran again; this time he won.

Bradley's first official act as a councilman was to move that Clarence Goodwin be fired. Nobody would second the motion, and that, pretty much, was the Bradley legislative history for the next two years.

"But I was learning," he says, chuckling impishly, "and by 1940 I had figured out what to do."

What he did was devise a plan to hobble

Goodwin and Bigley if he couldn't reform or remove them.

"I was not getting anywhere with the council, so I went to City Clerk John Lynch and took out a batch of initiative petitions. It was no trouble getting enough signatures to put five charter amendments on the ballot."

The most important of the five, probably, was the amendment cutting council terms from six years to four. A good portion of Charlie Bigley's power lay in the fact that San Joseans never could elect a majority of the council at any one election; the terms were staggered 3-2-2. That meant Bigley had only to concentrate on electing one, or at most two, council candidates every other year.

Bradley's amendment, which remained in effect until last year, staggered the terms 4-3. That gave San Joseans the opportunity to change city administrations every second election if they felt it necessary.

The other four amendments were aimed at giving the people a veto over the city manager and a check on his power to appoint and promote.

Bradley proposed that the city manager and the members of the city civil service commission be required to go before the people for a vote of confidence every two years and that civil service promotions be granted on the basis of written, rather than oral, examinations.

And, finally, just because Clarence Goodwin was pliable though honest, Bradley proposed that San Joseans create a five-member elected board of education with the power to appoint the superintendent of schools.

In April 1940, San Joseans bought the whole package except for the vote of confidence for the civil service commission, and that's how the San Jose Unified School District was born. It is a measure of Goodwin's basic honesty and good judgment (and Bigley's disinclination to "mess with the schools") that the new elected school board voted to keep Goodwin's superintendent of schools, Walter L. Bachrodt, on the job.

CLARK BRADLEY DIED DECEMBER 11, 1983, AT AGE 75.

John P. McEnery: Old Time Politician

April 28, 1981

If ever San Jose boasted a classic Irish politician, John P. McEnery, the father of San Jose City Councilman Tom McEnery, had to be it.

John was a native San Josean and he never spoke with an Irish brogue, but you always were waiting for him to. He looked and (except for the accent) sounded like a character from *The Last Hurrah* — big, bluff, plainspoken.

As he aged, his black hair turned a distinguished silver, but you couldn't say that advancing years mellowed him. John McEnery was born mellow, in the Irish manner, and he stayed that way all his life. He genuinely liked people, but he had few illusions about them. It's hard to hang onto illusions selling newspapers at Second and Santa Clara streets and working your way through college as (among other things) a gravedigger.

John McEnery's mellowness was one side of his keen appreciation of the human capacity for outrage.

He never held an elective office, although he ran twice — once for county supervisor and once for the Democratic nomination for state Assembly. John was the behind-the-scenes man who made the Democratic Party in Santa Clara County (and later in California) go in the days when being a Democrat here would get you a bus ride if you had a nickel.

John was what political writers like to call a wheelhorse. He chaired the committees that got things done, things like hiring the halls and filling them by cajoling party luminaries to speak. He saw to it that prospective voters got registered — and then voted. And for more than 40 years, he harrumphed at lazy or otherwise inept public officials and habitually poured more intensity and energy into more individual political campaigns than anybody else around.

It is almost inconceivable then, although Tom swears it to be gospel, that John McEnery got into politics by default.

"Dad was always athletic," Tom recalled the other day. "He mostly played basketball and baseball at St. Joseph's grammar school and later at Bellarmine, but when he entered the University of Santa Clara, for some reason, he went out

John P. McEnery. Mercury News photo.

for football. The first day he suited up, he tried to tackle Len Casanova (a bruising halfback and punt specialist who later became the Broncos' head coach) and wound up with a broken collarbone and two broken ribs. That's when he abandoned football for debate and political science."

It was a happy choice and characteristic of the pragmatic McEnery. He was always interested in what would work. Today people would call him *goal-oriented;* John just thought of himself as practical. It probably stemmed from his early upbringing.

John McEnery was born in 1906 in the family home at 13th and Julian streets. His father, Patrick H. *Mac*Enery (the family always insisted the spelling was a literary affectation) was an Irish journalist who came to the city editorship of the old *Mercury Herald* by way of London's Fleet Street. John may well have inherited his love of language from his father.

For whatever reason, Patrick *Mac*Enery's two boys went into the two most verbal professions, politics and the priesthood. (Father Henry Mc-

Enery, John's older brother, founded and was pastor of St. Albert the Great Church in Palo Alto at the time of his death in 1964.)

John grew up the way all youngsters did in small-town San Jose in the first quarter of this century. He went to school, sold papers downtown, played on school and neighborhood teams, took odd jobs (including, when he was older, the gravedigger chore for Tommy Monahan, the undertaker).

In fact, Monahan the undertaker may have played as large a role as Casanova the halfback in pushing John McEnery into politics. In the summer of his 19th year, John was toiling in Calvary Cemetery when he was struck by the most implacable of all nature's forces: love.

Leaning on his shovel momentarily, he espied Margaret Dolores Sellers placing flowers on an adjacent grave. She was, though he didn't know it then, the daughter of Benjamin (Honest Ben) Sellers, who was elected to the San Jose City Council in 1914 and who was one of those responsible for bringing the council-manager form of government to town.

Two years after John was graduated from the University of Santa Clara in 1930, and after he had established himself as manager of the Hotel Sainte Claire, John and Margaret Dolores were married. In addition to talking a lot of politics, they produced five children — three girls and two boys, of whom Councilman Tom is the youngest.

John McEnery's public life can be summed up quickly enough. He made his living in the home and hardware business, but his life was his family and politics, which latter activity gave full range to his talent for conviviality and invective. He loved the organizing, and he had no patience for guile or organizational deceit. He was as happy excoriating the City Council for the downtown "parking mess" (that council was, in McEnery's words, "a bunch of rumdums who don't know what's going on,") as he was taxing fellow Democrats for their moral laxity.

In the presidential election year of 1948, when McEnery was vice chairman of the California Democratic Party, he tangled bitterly with James Roosevelt, the eldest son of former President

Franklin D. Roosevelt. Jimmy wanted the California delegation to the Democratic National Convention to repudiate its pledged support of President Harry Truman; Roosevelt thought Gen. Dwight D. Eisenhower would pull better at the polls.

McEnery thought Roosevelt's opportunism "a damnable disgrace" and sought to block Roosevelt's nomination as Democratic national committeeman from California. "I have learned to hate him," said McEnery of Roosevelt, "because he has proved to be a hypocrite beyond doubt." Two years later, when Roosevelt ran for governor of California, McEnery supported Republican Earl Warren; hypocrisy was one trait McEnery couldn't abide in a politician.

That antipathy played a part, too, in his resignation from the one local office he ever held. In 1949 McEnery resigned from the San Jose City Planning Commission (after a two-year stint) because the City Council kept ignoring commission recommendations. "I don't want to belong to a city administration," McEnery said on that occasion, "where discontent and inefficiency are rampant."

In 1947, President Truman offered McEnery the superintendency of the United States Mint in San Francisco, but he turned the job down. In 1952, Truman appealed to John again, and this time McEnery acquiesced, knowing he wouldn't be there long. (In fact, he resigned in November of that year, shortly after Eisenhower was elected president.) That was as close as John McEnery ever came to political patronage; it was as close as he ever wanted to come.

For John McEnery, politics was more than expediency and winning elections. He loved a good fight, but he always had to know — and believe in — what he was fighting for. A yellowing clipping from the September 6, 1941 issue of *The Leader,* a Catholic weekly in San Francisco, makes the point in McEnery's own words.

Two months before Pearl Harbor, it was clear to everybody that the United States already was involved in World War II. Only the date and manner of formal entry remained in doubt, and it was in this atmosphere that McEnery addressed the state convention of the Ancient Order of Hibernians.

"You cannot defend a country," McEnery admonished his fellow Irishmen, "by raising armies and neglecting national morale! You cannot set out to conquer the world and leave behind a nation divided on all sorts of issues. You cannot work for a peace treaty pledging the brotherhood of man and the cooperation of nations when in your own land you enshrine class hatred, religious and racial prejudice, selfishness and greed and live by the principle, 'Every man for himself.' No! We need more than armies and industrial output. We must delve into the past and reappraise those qualities that have made this nation strong and great. A spiritual awakening is needed, a moral resurrection that will quicken a responsible citizenry. By this means alone can responsible nationalism reconstruct the world; by this means alone can that nationalism obtain and maintain peace . . .

"If worse comes to worst, America may very well be the last stronghold of freedom in the wide world.

"But this is the last ditch fight that every Irishman loves; he has been found with every forlorn hope for the last 1,000 years. As the tragic Gael once cried out:

'When the Kings of Eternal Evil
'Darken the Hills about,
'Our part — is with broken sabre
'To rise — on the last Redoubt."

That was John P. McEnery. Redoubtable.

How to Get Your Name on
a Journalism Building

September 23, 1981

Dwight Bentel could never stand still or sit still. At age 72 (he looks 55) he still can't. Bentel's nervous and intellectual energy is a marvel. The man bounces, swivels, spears ideas in midair with a punctuating forefinger. His blue eyes pierce; his once sandy hair, now iron-gray, still bristles electrically.

The first time I ever saw him, which was in the fall of 1949, he was punishing an office armchair unmercifully, rocking it back and forth at an estimated 120 RPM (rocks per minute), all the while cleaning his fingernails with a penknife and peppering me with pointed, not altogether congenial, questions:

Why did I think I wanted to be a newspaperman? What made me think I had any talent or aptitude for the calling? Didn't I know the field was underpaid and overcrowded? How did I propose to justify taking up a seat in his already jammed journalism department, a facility on its way to bursting as Uncle Sam freed his indentured nephews, the veterans of World War II?

I don't remember what I answered, but it must have been acceptable because I was spared the Bentel Rejection, which in those days comprised a handshake and directions to the industrial arts department. (Women of dubious prospect were advised to try their luck in home economics).

Even then Dwight Bentel was something of a legend. He had founded the journalism program at San Jose State College in 1934, with a single typewriter dog-chained to a desk in a cubbyhole office in a building that no longer exists. The Great Depression was in full flower, and Bentel was the whole faculty.

He hit the ground running (to use an expression favored by one of his later graduates, presidential counselor Lyn Nofziger), and he didn't stop for the next 40 years. By the time he retired, in 1974, Bentel had:

* Turned the occasionally issued College Times into the Spartan Daily, for 20 years, from 1934 to 1954, the only daily student newspaper in the California state college system.

* Introduced the first full-time journalism

internship program in the United States.

* Introduced the first four-year curricula in advertising, public relations, radio-television news and photojournalism on the Pacific Coast.

* Guided the Department of Journalism and Advertising (now Journalism and Mass Communications) to national accreditation in 1954, at the time one of only 47 schools in the nation.

Those are only some of the reasons the trustees of the California state college and university system this week named the San Jose State journalism building after him. It's a fitting tribute to a man who, among his other accomplishments, is the only non-publisher ever to be elected president of the California Newspaper Publishers Association.

In the past 46 years, San Jose State College (now University) has graduated perhaps 3,000 budding journalists; the present journalism-mass communications program enrolls more than 900 students. It's a big, and inevitably bureaucratic, operation.

But Dwight Bentel, who earned his doctorate in education from Columbia University in 1949 and says the exercise was worse than useless "because it represents time wasted," remembers the fun days, the mid-30s to mid-50s, "when we were bootlegging the school into something worthwhile."

"That's right, bootlegging," Bentel chuckled the other day as we sipped coffee in his wood-paneled Willow Glen living room. Do you know how I got our first 50 typewriters right after the war? I bootlegged 'em.

"We were enrolling kids like mad, but the state Department of Education wouldn't give us new equipment unless we had old, worn-out equipment to turn in for it. So I went to an Army surplus store and bought 50 mangled typewriters. They had no ribbons, most of the keys wouldn't work. I forget now what I paid for them, but they were just what I needed.

"I took off all the serial-number plates and turned in those beat-up hulks as worn-out equipment; the state Department of Education sent me 50 brand new typewriters in exchange.

"It was great," Bentel guffawed in recollection and then, sobering, added, "but the sad truth is you can't get away with that sort of thing anymore. Oh, you can still trim a little, swap equipment and supplies among departments — that's how we got the TV cables into the present journalism wing; they were science leftovers — but the bootlegging days are gone."

Gone, but not forgotten. To a great extent, the growth and expansion of San Jose State College to university status was a bootleg operation. The College's president from 1927 until 1952, Dr. Thomas W. MacQuarrie, was a pragmatist whose motto was "What I don't know can't hurt you." Dwight Bentel was to prove an adept pupil.

Dwight Bentel. **Mercury News photo.**

For most of Tom MacQuarrie's quarter-century at San Jose State, the school did double duty. It was both a state college and, under contract to the San Jose school system, a junior college as well. In consequence, whenever the state refused to give MacQuarrie money to launch a new department or expand an established one, the canny

81

old Scotsman did it anyway — as a junior college program, using junior college money.

If the program bombed, MacQuarrie buried it. If it flourished, he wrote it into his next proposed budget for submission to the state, which invariably took over its funding. Who can argue with success?

Such was the ambiance at San Jose State when Dwight Bentel arrived in 1934, fresh from Stanford with a double master's degree (in English and education). "My father always said we kids should have two strings to our bows."

Bentel senior taught chemistry at Commerce High in San Francisco, where Dwight and his older brother, Carr, were born and reared. Carr always wanted to be a doctor, and, in fact, retired a rear admiral after a career in the United States Navy Medical Corps. Dwight Bentel always wanted to be a newspaperman.

The year was 1928, and Prohibition, that Noble Experiment, was making hypocrites out of otherwise honest citizens and laying the foundations of organized crime's financial empire when Dwight Bentel got his first newspaper job, as copyboy on the old *San Jose Mercury-Herald*. He was 18 and fresh out of high school. The managing editor, Merle Gray, hired him because the Grays and the Bentels were friends and neighbors while Merle Gray was an assistant managing editor of the *San Francisco Examiner*.

"I'll never forget my first job at the *Mercury*," Bentel grinned. "I was given a desk right outside Merle Gray's office, just opposite the second floor elevator doors. They stuck a Civil War Colt's .45 hogleg in the desk drawer and told me to be very careful about who got in to see the editor." The *Mercury-Herald* publishers, "Red" and "Black" Hayes, had declared war on Demon Rum, and San Jose's bootleggers were nervous and not a little upset. Nobody ever tried to kill Merle Gray, but he wasn't inclined to take chances, in the office or not.

"Merle had a 12-gauge shotgun," Bentel recalled, "and I used to get a good grip on it and

slouch down in the back seat of his old touring car while he made the rounds of the bootleggers' retail outlets. Merle always wanted to know, first-hand, that he was getting the news straight."

The experience was to have a profound effect on the young man. It taught him that news belongs to the people, not to those who make it, and it stimulated his restless mind to endless speculation on the interdependence of journalism and the law. Ultimately, he became an authority on and author in the field of libel and communications law.

But that was to come later. First he had to work his way through Stanford University (as a correspondent for the *Mercury-Herald* at $25 a week), handle the public relations attendant on formation of the Santa Clara Valley Water Conservation District — and join the San Jose State faculty in 1934.

When World War II denuded the campus of students, Bentel took a leave (from 1942 to 1945) to work toward his doctorate at Columbia, financing himself by laboring in a New Jersey shipyard and later in the photography section of New York's Museum of Natural History. This latter experience led *Life* magazine to offer him a job as a photographer and the University of Illinois to offer him an assistant professorship in journalism. He turned both down. He did sign on with *Editor and Publisher* magazine, though, first as Chicago editor and later as education editor, a post he continued to hold for 17 years, even after he returned to San Jose and his first love — hammering the elements of libel and the sacredness of fact into the heads of would-be newsmen and newswomen.

Personally, I'll always consider Bentel's decision to come home one of my better strokes of luck.

AT 80, DWIGHT BENTEL IS AS PEPPERY IN RETIREMENT AS EVER HE WAS DURING HIS TENURE ON THE SAN JOSE STATE UNIVERSITY FACULTY. HE STILL LIVES IN SAN JOSE.

They Came for the Football Game
And Stayed for the War

December 7, 1981

Forty years ago this morning, at 7:55 Honolulu time, to be exact, 354 Japanese torpedo planes, dive bombers and escorting fighters, turned the United States naval base at Pearl Harbor into a flaming, oily junkyard.

In the space of two hours, the attackers killed 1,409 Americans, wounded 1,178 others, crippled the Pacific fleet and ushered the Unites States into a four-year war.

They also trapped the San Jose State College football team on the island of Oahu for 12 tension-ridden days.

The Spartans had arrived in Honolulu December 3 aboard the S.S. Lurline, the Matson Navigation Co.'s luxury flagship, to play three post-season benefit games. They left — well, all but seven of them left — December 19, weeks older but years wiser, in the steerage of the S.S. President Coolidge.

The war had caught the Coolidge enroute from Manila to Honolulu, and she was pressed into emergency service as a hospital ship return-

ing badly burned survirors of Pearl Harbor to San Francisco. The San Jose football players worked their passage home as unofficial ambulance attendants, gently hoisting the wounded soldiers and sailors on deck for daily lifeboat drills.

But between December 7, when the first bombs dropped, and December 19, when the first wartime convoy departed Honolulu for San Francisco, 30-odd San Jose State College football players, coaches and managers served as auxiliary members of the Honolulu Police Department. They were handed tin hats, riot guns and gas masks and instructed to make themselves useful.

For 12 days they enforced blackout regulations, guarded the Honolulu water works and assorted military installations, kept angry Hawaiians away from the Japanese consulate, reassured a jittery populace that The Invasion was not about to begin and dodged trigger-happy Hawaii Territorial Guardsmen in the dark. One Spartan even helped deliver a baby in a blackout on Pearl Harbor night.

Seven members of the team, police science majors for the most part, stayed on with the HPD

Newspaper photograph of San Jose State football team members embarking on their trip to Hawaii. Mercury News photo.

for three years before entering one or another branch of the military. The rest came home, to school and, in time, to military service.

Several members of that 1941 Spartan football team still live in the San Jose area, and three of them — Bert Robinson, Ken Stanger and Gray McConnell — reminisced the other day about their shared experiences of 40 years ago.

McConnell, now sales manager for a moving and storage company, undoubtedly had the best view of the war's opening salvo. It started with "waterspouts" off Waikiki.

"Allan Hardisty (now deceased) and I had left the Moana Hotel, where the team was staying, to walk along the beach," McConnell recalled, "because Al wanted to sneak a smoke, and Coach (Ben) Winkelman would have had his head for that. Then we saw these geysers of water spouting up from the Honolulu ship channel to the west. At first we thought they were waterspouts; then we realized they were bombs because we began to see the planes. We didn't know Pearl Harbor was being attacked because you can't see Pearl from Waikiki — Sand Island and Ahu Point get in the way."

That was just the beginning for McConnell, Hardisty and Charlie Cook, another team member also now dead. They'd had picnic plans for the day with a trio of University of Hawaii coeds, and now all the girls wanted to do, naturally enough, was get home. They lived in one of Honolulu's better residential neighborhoods, in the hills above and to the north of the naval base.

"But the main streets were already jammed with military traffic," McConnell went on, "so the girls directed us over the back roads, and at about 8:30 we found ourselves in the hills directly overlooking Pearl Harbor. The attack was still going on. We saw the planes diving, and the battleship Oklahoma capsizing and slowly sinking into the mud. The flames and the smoke from the Arizona cast a dirty brown pall over the whole scene. It was horrible, but it was fascinating, too. We stayed there the whole day, partly to see what more would happen and partly because the mother of one of the girls begged us to stay. She was *really* scared. Finally, the girl's father managed to get home late that afternoon, and he drove us back to the Moana about 6 pm. We'd been gone all day, and Coach Winkelman was furious. He didn't know whether we'd been killed or what."

Ken Stanger, who retired three years ago as principal of Lynbrook High School, was one of the seven Spartans who stayed in the islands as a policeman during the war's early years.

"People were terribly confused and jumpy at first," he remembers now, "and we weren't much better. That night (December 7) the HPD deputized us, sort of, issued us tin hats and riot guns, piled us into prowl cars and told us to douse any lights we could see. Nobody in Honolulu was used to the notion of blackouts yet.

"Thinking back now, I realize it was a miracle we didn't kill anybody. Even the regular police officers were jittery; my first night, the regular I was riding with arrested a woman because the pilot light on her water heater was showing. In those days, most Honolulu water heaters were located outdoors, and this lady lived up in the hills so the light from her heater could be seen from the sea. Hell, she was no spy; she was a Navy wife whose husband was at sea on a destroyer, but we booked her anyway."

It was Stanger who helped deliver the Pearl Harbor baby that first night.

"This lady called in — she didn't speak very good English, but we got the drift right away: She was in labor. It was well past curfew and full blackout was in effect. The regular HPD officer and I did the only thing we could do — we went out and helped her deliver. It was a baby girl, but I don't think they named her Pearl."

Bert Robinson, who coaches basketball and swimming at Prospect High School, was a 19-year-old sophomore — and the Spartans' star right halfback—that December 7. He, too, remembers the confusion, the tension, and yes, the excitement.

"Here we were, just a bunch of kids, really, but we grew up quickly, he recalls. "We had to. After riding around half the night in police cars, we had to take a bus from downtown Honolulu back to the Moana hotel on Waikiki beach. The second night out, some trigger-happy Territorial Guardsman put a .30-caliber slug through the bus when the driver didn't see his signal to stop. Nobody was hurt, but the Marine sergeant who officially 'commanded' the bus was highly indignant.

"There was a lot of indiscriminate firing that night and for the next few nights. Nobody got hurt that we ever heard of, but the Territorials bagged a cow in the rushes down by the Alawei Canal the night our bus was fired on."

The confusion wasn't much alleviated, but the bus rides got a bit safer when the team was relocated from the beachfront Moana Hotel to Punahou School, up the Nuuanu Valley away from downtown Honolulu. "The farther you got away from the beach, the less likely you were to be shot by a Territorial or some ROTC kid playing with live ammunition for the first time in his life," is the way McConnell remembers the move to Punahou.

And that's how it was for about 30 San Jose State College students 40 years ago today. They went to Hawaii to play football (a round-robin with Willamette and Hawaii Universities) and stayed for a war.

One of those who didn't go to Hawaii that December, Dwight Bentel, remembers with a touch of awe and disbelief even today — one who did; the late Sebastian "Scrappy" Squatrito.

In 1941, Bentel was head of the SJS journalism department; Squatrito was the senior manager of the football team and sports editor of the Spartan Daily. Day after day, Bentel and the Daily staff waited for Scrappy to file. They knew dispatches from Hawaii were now censored, and they expected a lot of oblique references to places and events when the Squatrito piece finally arrived. But they expected *something.* Here was Squatrito sitting on the biggest story of all time, and everybody knew he'd get something through."

But days turned into weeks. Nothing. The Spartans returned (on Christmas Day, 1941) and still no word from the silent sports editor.

Finally, Squatrito strolled into the Daily office the day after Christmas vacation ended, to be pinned against the wall, literally, by a breathless Bentel and crew.

"Scrappy," Bentel shouted, in a mixture of glee and vexation, "where's your story? Let's have it. You can forget the censors now."

Squatrito surveyed Bentel *et al* in astonishment. "What story?" he demanded indignantly. "There isn't any story. We never played those games. Haven't you heard? We're in a war."

BERT ROBINSON IS RETIRED FROM TEACHING NOW, AS IS KEN STANGER. GRAY McCONNELL IS STILL WITH HIS STORAGE AND MOVING COMPANY. DWIGHT BENTEL NEEDS NO UPDATING. THERE'S A SEPARATE PIECE ON HIM ELSEWHERE IN THIS BOOK.

What Really Happened to the Class of '32?

February 18, 1982

Times were hard in San Jose 50 years ago. The town was small (it had fewer than 60,000 residents), and economic opportunity, to say nothing of prosperity, was elusive. Nobody could find the corner President Hoover said it was just around.

Wall Street had gone belly up three years earlier, and the Great Depression was getting its teeth solidly into the American people. Of hope there was no lack, but it was tinged now with an air of resignation.

A particularly pretty (and judging from her yearbook photograph, intelligent) 1932 graduate of San Jose High School, Hazel Bell-Marie Mock, wrote in The Bell, the school's yearbook, that her ambition was "to be some boor's stenog."

She had a great deal of company that year; as the nation's economic horizons contracted, the sights of the Class of '32 seemed to drop commensurately. A job was a job; that was reality. Today, recognizing reality is called adjusting to an era of lowered expectations.

One who was not disposed to let the Class of '32 off so easily, however, was Raymond B. Leland, the SJHS principal and the man for whom today's Leland High School is named. Leland's message in the 1932 Bell was to prove prophetic.

"Soon," he wrote, "you are to pass out into a world where politics means much more than it has in your high school life. The sound class instruction and training you have received here in government should be a guide to you in your civic life, and if ever America needed clear thinking, intelligent and unwavering men and women it is at this time.

"You have been educated at considerable public expense. You in turn owe your community, state and nation the best that is in you, socially, economically and politically . . . It is for you to assume the responsibility of this leadership . . ."

On April 24, the San Jose High School Class of '32 will hold its 50th reunion in San Jose's favorite watering hole of the 1930s, the Sainte Claire Hotel, now undergoing renovation. How well have the members of the Class of '32

Don Edwards. San Jose High School Yearbook, 1932.

responded, over a half century, to the charge laid upon them by their principal?

You be the judge, but remember, in 1932 San Jose High School was the only educational game in a middling-small town, if you exclude a clutch of parochial and vocational schools. That year SJHS graduated about 550 young men and women, 217 of them in January, the rest in June.

Where are they now, and what did they do?

Some are dead, of course, and some have scattered across the country, but a surprising proportion of them still live right here. And they built this community, as Ray Leland told them they should.

The June class president was W. Donlon "Don" Edwards, whose ambition, according to The Bell, was "to play real golf." Instead, he went to Congress, where he serves today as chairman of the civil and constitutional rights subcommittee of the House Judiciary Committee.

Howard Walter Campen, whose enigmatic ambition was "to own a kiddy car," swapped a career in transportation for the law and government. He served as Santa Clara County counsel and, for 19 years after that, as county executive. He retired in 1976.

The class of '32 produced three San Jose city councilmen, two of whom, Robert C. Doerr and

Paul Moore, served terms as mayor. Ironically, the third councilman, Bill John Moore (no relation to Paul) told The Bell his ambition was "to be a mayor." He didn't make it, but he still lives here in The Villages; so a political comeback remains theoretically possible. Bob Doerr is still around, too, but Paul Moore died last September of a heart attack at age 66.

Vern Cristina (misspelled Christina in The Bell) wanted to be a fireman. Instead, he grew up to operate a warehouse and trucking company and to serve as chairman of the Santa Clara County Republican Central Committee and as a member of the California Highway Commission.

John Emil Longinotti wanted to become a lawyer, and he did. He is now Superior Court Judge Longinotti in Santa Clara County. John's brother, Eugene, also class of '32, wanted "to be a chemist," which he became, after a fashion. As a pharmacist, he operated a Willow Glen drug store for years.

On the other hand, Ralph Stuart Purdy wanted to be a police judge (perhaps because his father was a lawyer), but he became a doctor instead; he's been a practicing surgeon here since the end of World War II.

Ralph Goldeen, who just wanted "to enjoy himself," now runs the family furniture store in

Howard Campen. San Jose High School Yearbook, 1932.

downtown San Jose — and continues to contribute to downtown's renaissance.

The class of '32 produced its share of educators and school trustees, too, including Edwin Bruce Gould, who wanted "to look down on the Chrysler Building," but became an orchardist and manufacturer and, for a time, president of the Franklin-McKinley school board.

Bernard John "Barney" Watson wanted "to be a doctor," but retired, finally, as associate super-

Bernard Watson. San Jose High School Yearbook, 1932.

intendent of the San Jose Unified School District. (Restless in retirement, he signed on — and still serves — as executive secretary of the San Jose Rotary Club.)

Ray Leland's admonition notwithstanding, a few members of the Class of '32 scattered early and stayed away, the most notable, probably, being Merten Nocentelli. His professed ambition was "to play the harp," which, in fact, he may have learned to do. All that is known of him for certain, though, is that he changed his name to Wallen and went into the jewelry business in the Marshall Islands.

Then, there was Gordon Custer Leland, Ray Leland's son.

Gordon's ambition was to be a general, and, three weeks after his father died of a heart attack in 1933, Gordon Custer Leland entered West Point. He was graduated in 1937, won his pilot's wings at the Air Corps' Kelly Field and, by the time of Pearl Harbor, had risen to the rank of major.

On June 3, 1942, he was reported missing on a bombing mission along the China-Burma border. Months later, his mother thought she recognized him in a *Life* magazine picture of war prisoners interned by the Japanese in Singapore. Either she was mistaken, or Gordon Leland died in captivity. Officially, he is still missing/presumed dead.

Along with the majority of his classmates, Gordon Leland listened to his father's charge that he and they . . . "give the best that is in you." For the most part, they all did, and after a half century, their work — as doctors, lawyers, engineers, teachers, firefighters, police officers and yes, secretaries, stenographers, wives and mothers — is still with us, even if some of them, like Gordon Leland, aren't.

Contrary to popular misconception, San Jose did not spring full-grown from the brow of a silicon chip. It's an old town, and its roots go deep. Ask any surviving member of the San Jose High School Class of 1932.

DON EDWARDS IS STILL IN CONGRESS. HOWARD CAMPEN IS STILL RETIRED. JOHN LONGINOTTI RETIRED IN 1983 AND LIVES IN SARATOGA. VERN CRISTINA IS RETIRED AND LIVING IN SAN JOSE. BARNEY WATSON IS STILL WITH THE SAN JOSE ROTARY CLUB. RALPH GOLDEEN DIED IN 1984; BILL MOORE STILL LIVES IN THE VILLAGES. DR. RALPH PURDY IS NOW RETIRED AND LIVING IN SAN JOSE, AND EDWIN BRUCE GOULD, RETIRED, LIVES IN LOS BANOS. BOB DOERR IS STILL VERY MUCH WITH US AND IS DEALT WITH ELSEWHERE IN THIS BOOK.

Dreaming Along the Banks of the Guadalupe River

March 19, 1982

When you're broke you can afford to dream because that's about all you *can* afford. So maybe this is a good time for the city of San Jose and Santa Clara County to do a little creative dreaming about the Park of the Guadalupe.

City and county aren't precisely broke, but a deepening recession and Proposition 13 have dried up whatever spare cash either might have been willing to pump into new park development. Both governments worry, understandably, that every time they build a new park or fire station or library, they build higher operating costs into every annual budget after that.

Still, the dream of a Park of the Guadalupe persists. It's been included in official municipal planning documents at least since the end of World War II, but nothing has happened. The river was never anybody's Number 1 priority. That may be changing now.

With absolutely no fanfare, representatives of the city, the county, the Santa Clara Valley Water District, the San Jose Chamber of Commerce, and Lilyann Brannon of United New Conservationists, met February 3. They agreed, among other things, to set up some form of cooperative agency to develop the park and to create a streamside trail system through downtown. The details of this mechanism, and its funding, are still subject to negotiation.

Brannon, a 20-year resident of San Jose, has been dreaming about a Guadalupe River park for almost as long as she's been in town. Her United New Conservationists, an environmentalist umbrella group, has been cleaning up the river bed annually for almost a dozen years — and thereby lessening the stream's flood potential, as well as making it aesthetically more attractive.

Some weeks ago, she and I slipped and slid along muddy banks of the Guadalupe, tracing the route of the streamside trail that Ohlone Indians used for uncounted millenia. We saw, surprisingly, a kingfisher and a pair of snowy egrets less than a quarter mile from the financial high-rises of Park Center Plaza. We found also a remarkable variety of vegetation, some indigenous, such as the wild blackberry vines that probably nourished the Ohlones, and bamboo, probably brought in by the earliest Chinese immigrants.

As an urban park, the Guadalupe's downtown segment has real possibilities — hiking and riding trails, picnic areas, nature study sites. Where the Guadalupe's banks have been left more or less in their natural state, the river has created a genuine urban wilderness. The challenge is to preserve as much of the wilderness as prudence will permit, given the Guadalupe's penchant for occasional flooding, and to tame it for the common good. Brannon is convinced it can be done, and she is persuasive.

As we walked, she talked about her dream.

"Twenty years ago," she recalled, "my husband and I chose to live in San Jose because we found tree-lined streets, ivy-covered brick stone buildings on the San Jose State College (now university) campus, orchards, meandering creeks and access to the bay.

"We didn't know then that only a few years earlier San Jose had been designated the sixth most beautiful city in the United States. Imagine! And we hardly ever looked over the guardrail when we drove across the San Carlos Street bridge. The Guadalupe River was so tiny we didn't even notice it at first."

Brannon, a native of Baltimore, was to learn much, much more about the Guadalupe in the course of becoming a dedicated environmentalist. For openers, she discovered that the Guadalupe isn't just a misnamed creek.

"Yes," she went on, "it's officially a river because it has tributaries that feed into it, and it flows into San Francisco Bay. In fact, it has many similarities with the Jordan River (the Middle East stream that forms the boundary between Israel and Jordan). They're both about the same length and carry pretty much the same volume of water. The climate of the Jordan Valley is comparable to that of the Santa Clara Valley, and the original inhabitants of both valleys attached great spiritual meaning to their respective streams."

Warming to the subject, she went on: "The reason King Carlos of Spain established El Pueblo de San Jose de Guadalupe here in 1777 was because this little river supported the most abundant life found during the explorations of 1769. The Indians were handsomer, healthier and more numerous than any others encountered by the Spanish.

"The Ohlone Indians were apparently good traders as well as capable hunters and fishermen. Archeological finds along the Guadalupe suggest

Port San-Say on the Guadalupe River, c. 1910. San Jose Historical Museum collections.

they traded with tribes in the Pacific Northwest and with the Plains Indians as well. Mostly, they traded cinnabar, which the '49ers and the Chinese immigrants after them, coveted so.

"The Ohlones used to dig the cinnabar right out of the streambed, and what they didn't trade they painted on their bodies for ceremonial dances. For whatever it's worth, they probably got some dandy cases of mercury poisoning out of it, too."

Inching up the historical timeframe, Brannon recounted the Guadalupe's role in the rise and fall of San Jose as the first capital of American California.

"There's a plaque over on southeast Market Street, opposite the Old City Hall Plaza," she said, "that marks the location of the first California statehouse. King Carlos wasn't the only one who knew a good thing when he saw it. The Mexicans and the Americans also looked upon San Jose as a good place for a capital. It had everything: fertile land, a mild climate and plenty of water.

"Too much water in 1850-51, as it turned out. That winter, the skies opened up and dumped more than 32 inches of rain; the Guadalupe went over its banks and turned the Plaza area into a quagmire. The Legislature picked up its statutes and moved, first to Benicia and eventually on to Sacramento. When the weather improved, the Guadalupe returned to its normal channel, but the Legislature never came back."

Nor will it, in all likelihood; but the Guadalupe River remains.

We can, if we will, transform it from intermittent tiger to personal pussycat. The stream will probably never have enough sustained flow to permit boating or other water sports, but it can become a welcome retreat from the confining world of concrete and structural steel.

I think Lilyann Brannon's dream is worth sharing . . . How about you?

THOUGH FINANCING STILL REMAINS IFFY, THE CITY OF SAN JOSE UNDER MAYOR TOM MC ENERY, CONTINUES TO CHERISH PLANS FOR A CENTRAL PARK THAT WOULD INCLUDE THE DOWNTOWN PORTIONS OF THE GUADALUPE AS FAR NORTH AS SAN JOSE INTERNATIONAL AIRPORT. THE MASTER PLAN CALLS FOR A CONTINUOUS SYSTEM OF PATHS ALONG THE RIVER MAKING IT ACCESSIBLE TO WALKERS, JOGGERS, AND PICNICKERS. SOMEDAY, WHEN MONEY AND WILL MERGE — THE GUADALUPE MAY YET ACHIEVE ITS PARK POTENTIAL.

125 Years' Worth of Celebrating to do at San Jose State's Party

April 30, 1982

If my old alma mater, San Jose State College (now university) were casting about for a motto, it could do a lot worse than: You've come a long way, baby.

One hundred twenty-five years in the ed biz have left their mark on the school and on this community, which has been its home for 111 of those years. Today and tomorrow, San Jose State's Washington Square campus will be open to all comers. As a proud, if not particularly distinguished, graduate of the institution, I hope you'll drop by for a tour and for as many of the special events as will fit into your schedule.

The place, indeed, has come a long way.

A century and a quarter ago, a handful of young women, all of them teachers in San Francisco's fledgling public school system, enrolled in Minns' Evening Normal School to perfect their professional skills. In its scant five years of existence, Minns' graduated exactly 54 teachers, all of them women and all of them — alas — lost to history. There is no existing record of their identities.

This June, San Jose State University, the direct lineal descendant of Minns', will graduate about 4,000 students in the full range of arts and sciences; and, yes, the school will award credentials to approximately 500 teachers as well.

In historical terms, the metamorphosis of Minns' Evening Normal into San Jose State was no quickie caterpillar-butterfly affair. It was a lengthy, sometimes painful, and always political process. After 1862, when the state took over Minns' and renamed it California State Normal School, the politics became more pronounced. The move from San Francisco to San Jose, accomplished finally in 1871, is illustrative.

William Thomas Lucky, who succeeded George Washington Minns as principal of the Normal School, wanted to shelter his young charges from sinful temptation. San Francisco, he was convinced, was simply too big, too fast and too bright for proper young ladies, so he lobbied the Legislature ceaselessly to build a new school somewhere — anywhere but San Francisco. By 1870 he succeeded.

Lucky's next step was to find a community that would welcome his school, one that would appreciate its cultural and economic possibilities. A practical man, he took his sales pitch on the road, extolling the virtues of California State Normal School at each stop. In San Jose, he assured the assembled citizenry that the school would put their town on the map, making "the name San Jose synonymous with education as Stockton is synonymous with insanity." (Stockton was home to the state's insane asylum.)

Lucky clearly sold the editor of the *Mercury,* who told his readers two days later:

"Unlike a college or State University that attracts many fast and mischievous young men, not a desirable acquisition to the community, the Normal School comprises only the most desirable class of young people."

The San Jose City Council was sold, too. It offered the state Washington Square, the block bounded by Fourth, Seventh, San Carlos and San Fernando streets, as a campus site. The Legislature accepted, and in 1871, the California State Normal School came to town, never to leave.

In its 111 years here, it has grown in physical size, the number of students and academic scope. Today's main campus sprawls eastward to 10th Street and south of San Carlos, with aeronautical engineering facilities at San Jose Municipal Airport and an oceanographic research vessel based at Moss Landing. In recent years, the student body has stabilized at 24,500 undergraduates, and in 1972 the school achieved university status.

Shakespeare notwithstanding, there is considerable significance in names, and San Jose State's name changes over the years have reflected its physical growth and academic expansion. In 1921 it dropped the Normal School designation and became San Jose State Teachers College. In 1935 it expanded beyond "Teachers," becoming simply San Jose State College.

San Jose State College, 1941. San Jose Historical Museum collections.

In 1972, the Legislature re-created it California State University at San Jose, a name that was promptly and universally rejected by San Joseans. The school had been known simply as "San Jose State" for too many years; and in 1973, the Legislature rectified its gaffe, formally renaming the school, San Jose State University. The new name went on the official stationery January 1, 1974.

The university had matured as a major educational institution, and it is even more than that today. It is a source of strength, to its hometown and to the larger national and international community. Its graduates can be found — literally — all over the world and in every manner of profession and occupation.

As an old grad, that gives me a good feeling.

Happy 125th birthday, San Jose State, and many more of them.

THE OLD SCHOOL, 132 YEARS YOUNG NOW, IS STILL ALIVE AND KICKING ON WASHINGTON SQUARE.

Forty Years Later, Japanese-American Internees Fight for Justice

January 31, 1983

In the spring of 1942 Minoru Yasui was a young lawyer with a non-existent practice. Three months after the Japanese attack on Pearl Harbor hardly anybody in Portland, Oregon was hiring Japanese-American attorneys, and besides, the federal government was trying to throw him into a concentration camp.

That didn't strike lawyer Yasui as quite right. He'd committed no crime, except to be born of Japanese ancestry, and they had taught him at the University of Oregon law school that the military, even in wartime, has precious little authority over civilians.

So, late on the night of March 28, 1942 Yasui walked into Portland's downtown police station and demanded to be arrested for violating the 8 p.m. to 6 a.m. military curfew imposed on Japanese-Americans waiting to be shipped to one of the 10 relocation centers that would spring up from the Mojave desert to Arkansas.

"The cops tried to talk me into going home," Yasui, now director of Denver's Office of Community Relations, recalls. "They didn't want to arrest me and make waves. They had nothing against me, personally or professionally."

But Yasui insisted, and the cops obliged. It was the beginning of a legal odyssey that isn't over yet. Along the way, Yasui picked up company: Gordon K. Hirabayashi, a University of Washington student and a Quaker, and Fred T. Korematsu, an East Bay welder.

They had little in common except an intense aversion to being forcibly displaced from their homes, their jobs, their studies. As far as they understood it, the Empire of Japan was at war with the United States; they weren't.

Hirabayashi, the Quaker, felt most strongly about this. If he obeyed Executive Order 9066, the presidential directive excluding Japanese-Americans from the West Coast, he reasoned, he'd be admitting he was a spy. So Hirabayashi refused to be relocated.

As with Yasui, the civilian authorities felt uncomfortable about enforcing military orders. Instead of arresting Hirabayashi for refusing to be packed off to a relocation center, they nailed him

Japanese-Americans shown registering at San Jose State College gym prior to being sent to internment camps in wartime panic of the spring of 1942. Mercury News photo.

for the lesser offense of curfew violation; he'd been going to the university library every night to study.

Korematsu, then a welder by trade and now a draftsman living in San Leandro, had a couple of good reasons for not wanting to leave the Bay Area. First, he had a gut instinct that the government had no right to do this to him. Second, by early 1942 the Bay Area was already a major shipbuilding center. Work was plentiful, and the pay was good. So Fred Korematsu passed himself off as Spanish-Hawaiian and went to work in the shipyards.

The good life lasted until May, 1942 when he dropped into a bayfront drug store for a pack of cigarettes. He didn't look right to the suspicious clerk who called the cops.

Ultimately, their cases went to the top. In June, 1943 the U.S. Supreme Court upheld the military curfew in the *Yasui* and *Hirabayashi* cases. Eighteen months later, the court held in

Korematsu that "military necessity" indeed justified the forced mass evacuation of West Coast Japanese-Americans.

New evidence suggests the War and Justice departments knew long before 1943 that this rationale was hogwash and deliberately withheld that information from the Supreme Court. The evidence was uncovered by Peter H. Irons, a lawyer and professor of political science at the University of California, San Diego, who is researching a book on the wartime relocation. Armed with the Freedom of Information Act, Irons poked into govermnemt archives and came away with internal memos and uncensored draft reports that, he believes, undercut the government's case for "military necessity."

The court wasn't told, for example, that the Federal Bureau of Investigation and the Office of Naval Intelligence had examined and discounted the assertions of General J. L. DeWitt, the military commander on the West Coast, that Japanese-

Americans were engaging in espionage and sabotage. Further, naval intelligence and a secret State Department survey conducted before Pearl Harbor by Curtis B. Munson flatly contradicted DeWitt's initial assertion that, in any event, it was impossible to tell loyal Japanese-Americans from the disloyal.

That's why Yasui, Hirabayashi and Korematsu are asking federal courts in Portland, Seattle and San Francisco to reopen their cases. The say they wcrc railroaded, largely to spare the government the embarrassment of having to admit it had made a terrible mistake: that it had indiscriminately imprisoned 110,000 innocent citizens for no good reason.

Even before their cases reached the Supreme Court, however, it was clear the government was embarrassed and confused about the whole affair. It didn't seem to know whether to treat Yasui, Hirabayashi and Korematsu as errant children or dangerous trouble-makers. It had fewer doubts about Yasui, though; as a lawyer, he was a *real* troublemaker.

For example, the federal district court in Portland agreed with Yasui that in the absence of martial law the army can't order civilians around. But, it said, Yasui had lost his citizenship because his parents took him on a visit to Japan when he was nine years old and (proof positive of treason) before the war he had worked briefly as a lawyer for the Japanese consul general in Chicago.

Yasui was arrested in March, 1942, tried, convicted and sentenced to a year in prison and a $5,000 fine. He actually spent nine months shuttling between the Minidoka, Idaho, relocation center and the Multnomah County Jail in Portland while his case was being appealed. "Late in 1944," Yasui remembers, "they shoved me out of the gate at Minidoka with $25 and a bus ticket to Chicago."

By contrast, the Quaker Hirabayashi was found guilty of two counts of curfew violation and sentenced to 90 days in jail on each count, the sentences to run concurrently. Ironically, Hirabayashi bounced from one jail to another for

Japanese-Americans arrive at a Japanese internment camp in Manzanar, California, in 1942. Mercury News photo.

almost two years while he was appealing his case. He was finally freed in 1944 without ever having seen the inside of a relocation camp. Today, he's a professor of sociology at the University of Alberta in Canada.

Korematsu, the welder who evaded the relocation order, was found guilty and placed on five years probation. He spent 90 days in the Presidio of San Francisco stockade before being shipped to the relocation center in Topaz, Utah.

Ordinary Americans. Private citizens. Victims. Forty years later they're seeking justice.

They want to clear their names. And they want to destroy, for history and for the protection of future Americans, the *legal* basis that underpinned this nation's wartime concentration camps.

If they can do that — and I'm rooting for them all the way — they will have made it much harder for future courts to blandly accept the government's assertion that "military necessity" justifies telling any group of Americans the Constitution doesn't protect *them*.

BY THE LATE 1980s, FEDERAL COURTS IN SAN FRANCISCO, PORTLAND AND SEATTLE HAD VACATED THE WARTIME CONVICTIONS OF FRED KOREMATSU, GORDON HIRABAYASHI AND MINORU YASUI. YASUI DIDN'T LIVE TO ENJOY HIS VICTORY VERY LONG. HE DIED IN 1987.

CONGRESS PASSED H.R.442, THE LONG-OVER-DUE APOLOGY AND REPARATIONS BILL IN 1988 AND PRESIDENT REAGAN SIGNED IT BEFORE LEAVING OFFICE. UNFORTUNATELY, THE PRESIDENT DID NOT MATCH HIS SYMBOLIC GENEROSITY WITH HARD CASH, ASKING ONLY $20 MILLION FOR REPARATIONS IN HIS FINAL BUDGET.

AT THAT RATE, THE LAST SURVIVORS SHOULD BE COMPENSATED BY THE YEAR 2049, BY WHICH TIME ALL OF THEM WILL BE DEAD, OF COURSE. ONLY 50,000 OR SO CAMP SURVIVORS ARE STILL ALIVE IN 1989, AND MOST OF THEM ARE WELL PAST MIDDLE-AGE. FURTHER, THE JUSTICE DEPARTMENT ESTIMATED THEY ARE DYING AT THE RATE OF ABOUT 200 A MONTH. IN THIS MATTER, JUSTICE DEFERRED IS TRULY JUSTICE DENIED.

Bringing Back the Clang, Clang, Clang of Trolleys and Urchins

August 31, 1983

One of the avowed aims of the San Jose Trolley Corporation, subtitled a Historical Restoration Project, is to bring a little fun back downtown. Even a Calvinist would find it hard to be against the kind of fun the Trolley Corporation has in mind.

The corporation, a private, non-profit organization headed by Santa Clara County Supervisor Rod Diridon, who doubles as chairman of the County Transit District, wants to restore a half-dozen 30-passenger California-type trolley cars and run them over Transit District light-rail tracks in downtown's future transit mall.

In addition to providing a valuable shuttle service for shoppers, lunchers and folks who work downtown, the cars — probably painted in traditional canary yellow and maroon — would add a touch of color and dash and tickle the nostalgia nerve-ends of oldtimers. Two of the cars the Corporation proposes to restore, the 124 and the 73, actually bounced and rumbled over San Jose streets until 1938, when the last tracks were torn up and the motorcoach reigned supreme.

The Trolley Corporation has kicked off a $1.5 million fund drive for the restoration, headed by Bob Hosfeldt, general manager of Gill Cable TV. I wish the effort luck. Whatever else they may be, trolleys are fun. Take it from an ex-kid who rode plenty of them in the course of misspending a Depression-era youth. Many and happy were the hours spent in, on and around the big California-type cars of the old Market Street Railway in San Francisco and the smaller but much more exotic Birneys that in the late 1930s constituted the transportation backbone of such places as Fresno, Stockton, Sacramento and, to a lesser degree, San Jose.

The Birney, named for its designer Charles O. Birney, was a 25-foot galloping birdcage that served as the inspiration for Fontaine Fox's Toonerville Trolley cartoons. Fox grew up in Louisville, Kentucky, where the Birneys were in vogue before World War I.

Indeed, transportation engineer Birney threw his contraption together in response to the prewar slump that was threatening to drive many

California-style car #72 eastbound on Santa Clara approaching the underpass near Stockton Avenue in the early 1930s. San Jose Historical Museum collections.

street railways to the wall. They wanted a machine that was cheaper to run, and Birney obliged them with a smaller car that could be operated by one man, a combination motorman-conductor, instead of the usual two-man crews on the larger trolleys.

But Birney not only shortened the car and cut its overhead in half. In a stroke of something less than genius he decided to plunk it down on a single truck, or set of four wheels, positioned in the center of the chassis. As a result, the Birney took on some of the operating characteristics of a see-saw. It would dip and rise, dip and rise, rhythmically, with every deviation of the tracks from dead-level.

Irreverant youngsters of that era amused themselves endlessly by jumping on the rear of the car (the rear was the end where the motorman-conductor wasn't at the moment) and, holding fast to the trolley pole's guy wire, rocking the car up and down. The ultimate object of the game was to dislodge the trolley pole from the overhead wire that supplied the power.

Once the trolley pole pulled free, the Birney would coast to a halt (or it would stop a lot faster if the motorman took his foot off the dead-man control, which he almost always did in these circumstances), and the operator would descend, usually screeching dire threats at the retreating vandals, to reposition the trolley pole. If the pranks were too frequent, and if they were concentrated on a single line, they could play havoc with the timetable, but as a rule they were more an annoyance to the operators than a threat to the safety or convenience of the passengers.

In a couple of respects, though, the Birneys were less fun than the California cars. An urban urchin looking for a free ride was out of luck with a Birney; its skin was smooth, and it lacked convenient handholds. The California car, so named because its two ends were open to California's unfailing sunshine and fresh air, offered eager hands all manner of wires, cow-catchers and railings to grasp. Also, when times got really tough, the Californias were operated by a single motorman-conductor, and he was a long, long way from the end of the car where the ride-hitchers clung precariously. A firm grip usually guaranteed a completed ride.

In one other respect, the Californias provided mean little kids with superb fun. The cars, which could and sometimes did attain speeds of 50 miles an hour, became rolling mills at high speed. They could flatten, elongate or otherwise distort any small metal object placed on the track. Bottlecaps were a favorite, but the top of the line in this caper was the Lincoln head penny, which was moderately hard to come by in those years. The scam usually worked this way:

Urchin A would produce a previously smashed penny; one on which the Lincoln looked like Mr. Five-by-Five or a professional basketball center, and ask Urchin B how he'd like one, too. Urchin B, almost invariably broke, would concede he'd sure like to have one. Whereupon Urchin A would produce an unsmashed penny and, in a burst of camaraderie, offer to put it on the tracks for Urchin B, who was thrilled, impressed and grateful.

Soon, a big California car would come racket-

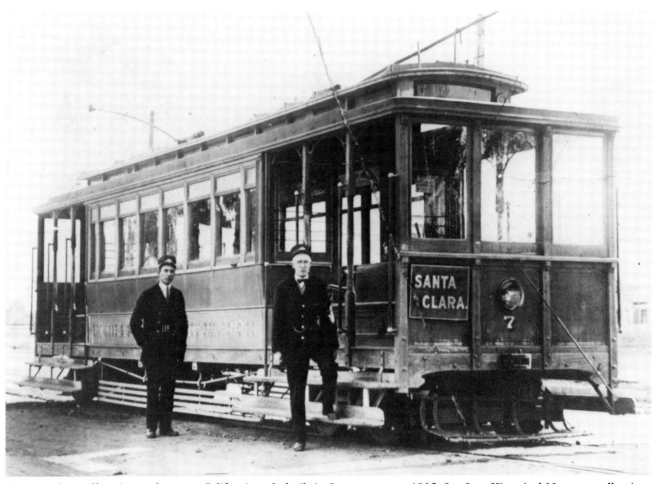

San Jose-Santa Clara interurban car, California-style built in Sacramento, c. 1905. San Jose Historical Museum collections.

ing down the tracks (the scam was always worked in mid-block to guarantee optimum operating speed) and smash the penny. Urchin A would clap Urchin B on the back and urge him to collect his trophy. Urchin B would pick up the newly-smashed Lincoln head — and drop it immediately with a howl of pain. It was *hot,* having just been mill-rolled by several tons of hurtling trolley car.

Thus did Urchin B learn an unforgettable lesson in applied physics, one that he felt duty-bound to pass along to Urchin C as soon as he could find a couple of pennies and someone more gullible than himself.

I'm pulling for the San Jose Trolley Corporation to get those California Cars back on the track here. I never did find an Urchin C.

THE FIRST TWO RESTORED TROLLEY CARS (CALIFORNIA TYPE #124 AND #129) WENT INTO SERVICE ON THE DOWNTOWN TRANSIT MALL PORTION OF THE GUADALUPE CORRIDOR LIGHT RAIL SYSTEM IN NOVEMBER 1988. A THIRD CAR, CALIFORNIA TYPE #73, WAS ADDED IN MAY 1989. THREE MORE CARS ARE IN THE PROCESS OF RESTORATION IN THE TROLLEY RESTORATION BARN AT THE SAN JOSE HISTORICAL MUSEUM.

Foltz for the Defense

December 23, 1984

Clara Shortridge Foltz isn't exactly a household name in San Jose, not even among lawyers, but she ought to be. By next spring she will be, if Santa Clara County Public Defender Sheldon Portman has his way.

Clara Foltz, who died in Los Angeles in 1934 at age 85, was a schoolteacher, dressmaker, mother of five, divorcee and California's first woman lawyer.

She was admitted to the bar in a San Jose courtroom on September 5, 1878, and practiced here for a half-dozen years before moving on to San Francisco and, later, Los Angeles. She had to fight the legal profession and the California Legislature just to call herself a lawyer, which would be reason enough to remember her.

Portman has another motivation for refurbishing her memory just now. Next April marks the 20th anniversary of the Santa Clara County Public Defender's office. Portman has been lobbying, with some initial success, to have 1985 designated the centennial year of the public defender

movement in the United States and Clara Foltz recognized as its principal architect.

Clara Shortridge Foltz was a suffragist, a prison reformer, a political activist who helped elect her brother Samuel M. Shortridge to the U.S. Senate, a lecturer and a contributor of articles to law reviews and to her brother Charles Shortridge's newspaper, the *San Jose Mercury*.

She was also a headstrong girl who, at age 16, gave up a teacher's job in Illinois to elope with Jeremiah Foltz, a young man of slender prospects and a thirst for travel. In the course of a dozen years, they bounced from Illinois to Oregon to San Jose where, in 1874, Jeremiah sold real estate and tended a small grocery store while Clara tended their two boys and three girls.

By 1876, Clara had had enough of domesticity. She divorced Jeremiah and announced to the assembled Shortridges, who had moved to San Jose by then, that she intended to study law. They were encouraging; the bar was not.

There was no law school in San Jose, and the first lawyer she sought to apprentice herself to, Francis Spencer, offered to help her get back into

Clara Shortridge Foltz. San Jose Historical Museum collections.

school teaching. Ultimately C. C. Stephens, who operated what he modestly described as a "neighborhood law office," allowed her to read law with him. Perhaps he wondered why: Section 275 of the code of Civil Procedure restricted the practice of law in California to "any white male citizen."

Undaunted, Foltz badgered State Senator Barney Murphy, D-Santa Clara, to introduce a bill repealing the racial and sexual limitations. Nobody seemed to mind the race part; sex was something else, as Foltz was to recall years later.

"The bill," she wrote 40 years later, "met with a storm of opposition such as had never been witnessed upon the floor of a California Senate. Narrow-gauge statesmen grew as red as turkey gobblers mouthing their ignorance.... and staid old grangers who had never seen the inside of a courthouse seemed to have been given the gift of tongues." After two years of heated debate, on and off the floors of the Legislature, the Murphy-Foltz bill became law, and Clara Shortridge Foltz

passed the 20th District Court bar in San Jose and became California's first woman lawyer.

It was only the beginning.

With all due respect to C. C. Stephens, Foltz thought she needed further legal tutoring and enrolled in the Hastings College of Law in San Francisco. It took the Hastings' trustees two days to realize what had happened, whereupon they unanimously adopted a resolution "that women be not admitted to the Hastings College of Law" and threw her out.

She sued in the California Supreme Court, arguing that if women had a legal right to be lawyers, they couldn't be barred from law school, especially a public law school. She won — for herself and for all 12,000 women attorneys practicing in California today.

Meanwhile back at the bar, in San Jose, Clara probated wills, handled divorces and learned first-hand how the cards were stacked against criminal defendants without money to hire a lawyer. The court appointed counsel in these cases, usually with results disastrous to the defendant.

Appointed attorneys had no time to prepare a defense, no money for investigators to locate witnesses; and almost always, they were outclassed by the paid, professional prosecutor.

"The appointees," Clara observed, "come from failures in the profession, who hang about courts hoping for a stray dollar or two from the unfortunate, or from the kindergartens of the profession just let loose from college and anxious to learn . . ."

"The remedy . . . lies in the election or appointment of a public defender . . . chosen in the same way and paid out of the same fund (as the public prosecutor)." Under such a system, she insisted, "malicious prosecution would cease, the accused would have an adequate defense, trials would be judicial inquiries, courts would be freed from the squabbles that now disgrace them, the profession would be relieved from the burden of compulsory services and the expense would fall on the state at large, where it . . . belongs."

So saying, she drafted a model public defender bill and, by 1893, had personally secured its introduction in 32 state legislatures. The California Legislature finally adopted the Foltz Defender Bill, virtually intact, in 1921.

Not content, Clara Foltz wrote the bill creating California's first parole system. She persuaded the San Francisco County supervisors to stop confining prisoners in iron cages in the courtroom, and she got the county to segregate juveniles from adults in the county jail.

Having railed for years against the excesses of conviction-hungry district attorneys, Clara decided to try for a cure from the inside. In 1910, at the age of 61, she accepted appointment as a deputy district attorney of Los Angeles County. She was the first woman to hold that job.

A year later, she wrote an amendment to the California constitution giving women the vote "at all elections." She campaigned for the initiative, and the voters enacted it in November 1911.

Foltz never got around to writing her autobiography, but she did pause long enough, in 1918, to jot this down:

"Everything in retrospect seems weird, phantasmal and unreal. I peer back across the misty years into that era of prejudice and limitation, when a woman lawyer was a joke . . . but the story of my triumphs will eventually disclose that though the battle has been long and hard-fought it was worthwhile."

THANKS TO SHELLY PORTMAN, WHO LEFT THE PUBLIC DEFENDER'S OFFICE IN DECEMBER, 1986 TO ENTER PRIVATE LAW PRACTICE IN SAN JOSE, 1986 *WAS* DESIGNATED THE CENTENNIAL OF THE PUBLIC DEFENDER MOVEMENT IN THE UNITED STATES. IN CONNECTION WITH THE CENTENNIAL, THE AMERICAN BAR ASSOCIATION AND THE NATIONAL LEGAL AID AND DEFENDER'S ASSOCIATION ESTABLISHED THE CLARA S. FOLTZ AWARD WHICH ANNUALLY HONORS AN OUTSTANDING PUBLIC DEFENDER PROGRAM IN THE UNITED STATES.

Index

Agnew State Hospital, 38, 69
Ahu Point, 84
Airport Commission, 26
Airport Village, 57
Alameda County, 47
All American City, 11
Allen, Charles Sumner, Sr., 58, 59
Almaden Avenue, 49
Almaden Dam, 4
Almaden Road, 49
Alum Rock, 54
AME Zion Church, 19
American Municipal Association, 61
Ancient Order of Hibernians, 79
Anderson Dam, 5
Ann Arbor, 74
Anti-Defamation League of B'nai B'rith, 13
Antioch Baptist Church, 20
Arizona, 84
Atlanta, Georgia, 44
Attaway, Karen, 7
Avrech, Anna, 12
Avrech, Ben, 11, 12, 13
Avrech Henry, 12
Avrech Family, 12
Bachrodt, Walter, 76
Bank of the West Building, 7
Barron Gray Packing Co., 16, 17
Battleship Oklahoma, 84
Bay Area, 62, 96
Beck, Joe, 5
Bellarmine, 77
Benicia, 91
Bennett, Grant R., 58, 59
Bentel, Carr, 82
Bentel, Dwight, 80, 81, 82, 85
Berkeley, 47
Berryessa District, 2
Biblioteca Latino Americana, 27, 28, 29
Bigley, Charlie, 25, 42, 43, 75, 76
Birmingham, Alabama, 45
Birney, Charles O., 99

Birneys, 99, 100
Bissell, Dr. Dwight Montgomery, 59, 67, 68, 69
Black, Police Chief John N., 25
Blackmore, John Raymond "Ray", 42, 43
Blind Center, 45
Bonanno, Frank, 51
Bradley Farm in Coldwater, Michigan, 74
Bradley, Clark L, 73, 74, 75, 76
Bradley, Howard, 74
Bradley, Mae & Glenn, 74
Bradley, Mae Clark, 73
Brannon, Lilyann, 64, 89, 90, 91
Brosseau, Col. & Mrs. D. I., 45
Butchers' Union, 34
Calero Dam, 4
California Cars, 100, 101
California Highway Commission, 87
California Newspaper Publishers Association, 81
California Prune & Apricot Growers Association, 10, 66
California State Library, 27
California State Normal School, 92, 93
Calvary Cemetery, 78
Cambrian School, 9
Camp Ord, Monterey, 30
Camp McQuaide, Watsonville, 30
Campbell, Orvin W. "Hump", 26, 46, 47, 48
Campbell, William, 4
Campbell, 15, 61
Campbell School District, 71
Campen, Howard Walter, 87
Canoas Creek, 51
Carlyle Street, 32
Carmelite Monastery, 53
Carter, Ben, 25, 47
Casanova, Len, 78
Cassell, Beverly, 45
Cassell, David, 45
Cassell, Dr. Irving, 45
Cassell, Sylvia, 44, 45
Cassin, R., 75
Center For The Performing Arts, 52
Centerville, 15

Central Valley, 34
Champion, Bill, 67
Chatton, Dr. Milton J., 39
Chavez, Cesar, 34
Children's Discovery Museum, 52
Chynoweth, T. B., 65
City College, 15
City Hall Plaza, 30, 31
Civic Auditorium, 20, 52
Clark, Paul Fenimore, 58, 59
Cleaves Avenue, 2
Climax, Michigan, 73, 74
College of the Pacific, 58, 59
College Times, 80
Columbia, 82
Columbia University, 33, 81
Commerce High, San Francisco, 82
Conte, Nora Sepulveda, 29
Cook, Charlie, 84
Cooper, Louise, 9
Cory, Dr. Andrew Jackson, 39, 40
Cory, Dr. Benjamin, 39, 40
Cottage Grove, 49, 50
County Hospital, 50
County Medical Society, 68
County Transit District, 99
County Water District, 5
Covill, Dorothy, 75
Coyote Creek, 26
Coyote Dam, 4
Coyote River, 5
Cristina, Vern, 87
Crystal Springs Gap, 23
Cupertino, 14
Dallas, Texas, 8
Davies, Pierce, 59
Delmas Street, 14
Del Monte Cannery, 17
DeWitt, General J. L., 96, 97
Diablo Range, 21, 22
Dimas, 49, 50
Diridon, Santa Clara County Supervisor Rod, 99
Doerr, Charles, 60
Doerr, Fred, 61
Doerr, Phillip, 60, 61
Doerr, Robert C. "Bob", 60, 61, 63, 75, 87
Doerr, Mrs. Robert C., 62
Dole Hawaiian, 16
Donner Party, 24
East San Jose, 20, 43
East Santa Clara Street, 53
Eastern Europe, 12
Eastridge, 53
Eden Vale, 65
Edenvale, 65
Edenvale Historical Landmark District, 64
Editor & Publisher Magazine, 82
Edmonson, Jim, 37
Edwards, W. Donlon "Don", 87
Eisenhower, Gen. Dwight D., 79
El Pueblo de San Jose de Guadalupe, 90
Elks Club, 20
Empire of Japan, 31, 95
England, 9
Europe, 56
Evergreen, 54
Executive Order 9066, 95
Farmers Educational & Cooperative Union, 10
Farmers Insurance Group, 10
Federal Reserve Act, 66
Fifth Street, 17
First Street, 4, 54, 55
First & Santa Clara Streets, 54, 73
First National Bank Building, 76
Fischer, Clyde, 68, 69
Foltz, Clara S. Award, 104
Foltz, Clara Shortridge, 102, 103, 104
Foltz, Jeremiah, 102
Foltz Defender Bill, 104
Fontaine Fox's Toonerville Trolley, 99

Fort Dix, New Jersey, 56
Fountain Alley, 4
Fourth Street, 19, 61
Fourth Ward, 24
Fox Theater, 24
Franklin Street, Santa Clara, 53
Fresno, 68, 99
Fresno State College, 68
Frontier Village, 64, 65
Fuhrerbunker, 61
Galarza, Ernesto & Mae, 33
Galarza, Dr. Ernesto, 33, 34
Garden City Women's Club, 20
Gardner School, 28
Gardner-Alma Neighborhood, 27
Garrod, David, 9
Garrod, David & Sophia, 9
Garrod, R. V. "Vince", 9, 10
Garrod, Richard S. "Dick", 9, 10
Garrod, Vincent S., 9, 10
Garrod Boulevard, 10
Garrod Farm, 10
Garrod Farm Stables, 10
Garrods of Saratoga, 9, 10
Germany, 24, 60, 61
Gill Cable TV, 99
Gold Placero, 39
Goldeen, Ralph, 87
Golden Gate, 23
Good Government League, 66
Goodwin, Clarence B., 25, 42, 43, 76
Goosetown, 49
Gould, Edwin Bruce, 88
Grant Street, 49, 50
Gray, Merle, 82
Graystone Lane, 22
Guadalajara, Jalisco, 49
Guadalupe Creek, 50
Guadalupe Dam, 4
Guadalupe River, 24, 89, 90, 91
Hamann, City Manager "Dutch", 69, 75
Hammer, Phil, 30
Hardisty, Allan, 84
Hartford Avenue, 57
Hastings College of Law in San Francisco, 73, 103
Hathaway, Parker, 75
Hawaii, 84, 85
Hayes, Anson E., 65
Hayes, Everis Anson "Red", 65, 66, 82
Hayes, Jay Orley "Black", 65, 66, 82
Hayes Mansion, 65, 66
Hayes-Chynoweth, Mary Folsom, 64, 65
Hayes, President Rutherford B., 65
Hayes Family, 65, 66
Heintze, Carl F., 70
Heinz, Gloria, 29
Herbert Hoover Junior High School, 60
Highway 17, 36
Hirabayashi, Gordon K., 95, 96, 97, 98
Historical Restoration Project, 99
Hitler, Adolph, 61
Holy City, 36, 37, 38
Holy City Post Office, 38
Holy City Print Shop, 36, 37
Honey Lake, 9
Honolulu, 7, 83, 84, 85
Honolulu Police Department, 83
Hosfeldt, Bob, 99
Hotel Sainte Claire, 78
Hubbard, Dr., 45
Human Relations Commission, 13
Human Relations Committee, 61
Humane Society, 51
Imperial Valley, 34
Irons, Peter H., 96
Jackson, Agnes, 20
Jackson, Inez C., 19, 20
Jackson, Leon, 19, 20
James, Superior Court Judge William F., 59
Japanese-Americans, 96, 97

Johnson, Dr. Samuel, 59
Jones, Herbert C. "Herb", 3, 4, 5, 6
Jordan River, 90
Jordan Valley, 90
King Carlos of Spain, 90, 91
Kissel, Emil, 8
Knight-Ridder, 66
Knowles, Dr. Tully, 59
Korematsu, Fred T., 95, 96, 97, 98
Langston University, Langston Oklahoma, 20
Lanini, Edwin, 45
Lassen County, 9
Latin-American Library, 28
Leland, Gordon Custer, 88
Leland, Raymond B., 86, 87, 88
Leland High School, 86
Levitt, Jose, 30
Lexington Dam, 5
Lincoln Avenue, 53
Lisher, Velma, 64
Lively, James, 25, 47
Lockheed Missiles & Space Co., 36, 72
Locust Street, 27
Lodi, 47
Long, George, 50
Longinotti, Eugene, 87
Longinotti, Judge John Emil, 87
Lopez, Dr. Dan C., 49, 50
Los Angeles County, 104
Los Altos, 65
Los Angeles, 102
Los Gatos, 5, 14, 36, 54
Los Gatos Creek, 5
Louisville, Kentucky, 99
Lourdeaux, Dr. Stanley, 65
Lowell Grammar School, 74
Lucky, William Thomas, 92, 93
Lynbrook High School, 84
Lynch, City Clerk John, 76
MacEnery, Patrick H., 87
MacQuarrie, Dr. Thomas W., 59, 81
Manson, Dr. R. Morton, 70, 71, 72
Manson, Mrs. R. Morton, 71
Manzanar, 97
Mariposa, 39
Market Street, 24, 53, 91
Market Street Railway in San Francisco, 99
Martha Street, 17
Marysville, 34
Mayfair, 53
Mayfair Department Store, 12, 13
McBeth, Donna, 8
McCabe, Jay, 30
McConnell, Gray, 84, 85
McDonald, Bruce, 57
McEnery, Father Henry, 78
McEnery, John P., 77, 78, 79
McEnery, Mayor Tom, 91
McEnery, Tom, 77, 78
McKenzie, Charles, 31
Mendez-Ortiz, Linda, 29
Menlo Park, 15
Menlo School and College, 15
Mercury Herald, 58, 59, 66, 78
Michigan, 65, 74
Michigan State, 15
Milpitas, 61
Mineta, Representative Norman Y., 66
Minidoka, Idaho, 97
Minns, George Washington, 92
Minns Evening Normal School, 92
Moana Hotel, 84, 85
Mock, Hazel Bell-Marie, 86
Moffett Field, 30, 31
Monahan, Tommy, 78
Monte Bello Ridge, 9, 10
Moore, Bill John, 87
Moore, Paul, 87
Moss Landing, 93

Mother Lode, 14, 1
Mountain Echo, 36, 37
Mr. San Jose, 11
Multnomah County Jail, Portland, 97
Munich, 61
Munich: Culprit or Scapegoat, 61
Municipal Airport, 25
Munson, Curtis B., 97
Murphy, Barney, 103
Murphy, Lou, 36, 37
Murphy-Foltz Bill, 103
N. Bascom Avenue, 44
National Association for the Advancement of Colored People, 20
National Farm Workers Union, 33, 34
National Historic Register, 65
National League of Cities, 61
Nebraska, 58
Nevada City, 14, 15, 39
New Almaden Quicksilver Mines, 50
New York Bakery, 60
New York City, 45
New York's Museum of Natural History, 82
Nissen, Jim, 26
Nocentelli, Merten (Wallen), 88
Nofziger, Lyn, 80
Norman, Charles, 36
North First Street, 5, 67
North Market Street, 67
Nuuanu Valley, 85
Nyman, Marilyn, 26
O'Brien, Lester, 48
Oahu, 83
Oak Hill Memorial Park, 39, 43
Oak Street, 51
Oakdale, 36
Oakland, 20, 27, 62
Ohlone Indians, 90, 91
Okayama Prefecture, 62
Okayama, Japan, 61
Old City Hall Plaza, 91
Orchard Avenue, 50
Orchard Street, 49, 50, 51
Orozco, Joes Luis, 28
Owens, Vic, 75
Pace, Councilman Joseph, 69
Pacheco Pass, 3
Pacific Ocean, 21
Page, George W., 65
Palm Street, 27
Palmer, Carl W., 57
Pan-American Union, 34
Parent-Teacher Association, 20
Park Center Plaza, 89
Park of the Guadalupe, 89
Pasadena, 47
Pearl Harbor, 83, 84, 85, 95, 97
Perfect Christian Divine Way, 36
Pettit, Russ, 30
Peyton, Jewel, 16
Peyton, Wesley G., 2
Pioneer High Schools, 15
Plummer, Fire Chief Charles, 25
Police Activities League, 43
Portland, Oregon, 95, 97
Port San-Say, 90
Portman, Sheldon, 102
Portman, Shelly, 104
Potter's Field, 50
Presidio of San Francisco, 98
Prospect High School, 85
Prussia, Leland, 30
Pueblo de San Jose, 39
Punahou School, 85
Purdy, Dr. Ralph Stuart, 87
Quest Club, 58, 59
Redwood Estates, 36
Reed, Frazier O., 24
Reed, James Frazier, 24
Reichsteiner, Emil, 37

Renzel, Ernest H. Jr., 24, 25, 26, 47
Richmond, 19
Riegel, Dr. Christopher A., 21
Riker, "Father" William Edward, 36, 37, 38
Rio Grande Industries, 65
River Park Towers, 52
Robinson, Bert, 84, 85
Roosevelt, President Franklin D., 79
Roosevelt, James, 78
Roosevelt, Teddy, 58
Rossi, Louis, 32
Rossmoor, 48
Route 17 Freeway, 25
Rowan, Dr. Robert, 71
Roy, Dr. & Mrs. David, 31
Rozum, Stephen "Rosie", 37
Ruffo, Albert J., 25, 47, 75
Rundle, Roy, 25
Russia, 12
Ruth's Revolt, 59
S.S. President Coolidge, 83
S.S. Lurline, Matson Navigation Co., 83
Sacramento, 10, 33, 73, 75, 91, 99, 101
Sacramento Bee, 33
Sacramento High School, 20
Sacramento River, 3
Sacramento River Delta, 5
Sacramento Valley, 22
Sacred Heart Church, 27
Sainte Claire Hotel, 86
San Antonio Street, 19
San Benito County, 3
San Bruno Gap, 23
San Carlos Street, 90
San Diego, 34, 47, 48
San Felipe, 5
San Felipe Project, 3
San Fernando Street, 17, 54
San Francisco, 8, 36, 62, 75, 76, 79, 83, 92, 102
San Francisco Bay, 4, 90
San Francisco Examiner, 82
San Joaquin Valley, 22, 36
San Jose, 7, 8, 11, 12, 13, 15, 16, 19, 20, 24, 25, 26, 27, 30, 33, 46, 49, 50,
56, 58, 61, 62, 66, 67, 73, 74, 89, 90, 91, 92, 93, 99, 102
San Jose Board of Education, 58
San Jose Brewery, 61
San Jose Chamber of Commerce, 89
San Jose City Planning Commission, 79
San Jose Community College District, 15
San Jose Convention Center, 52
San Jose, Costa Rica, 61
San Jose Evening News, 66
San Jose Fire Department, 11
San Jose Health Department, 68
San Jose Herald, 66
San Jose High School, 15, 42, 74, 76, 86, 87
San Jose High School Class of 1932, 88
San Jose Human Relations Commission, 11, 20
San Jose International Airport, 91
San Jose Mercury, 66, 102
San Jose Mercury-Herald, 82
San Jose Municipal Airport, 57, 93
San Jose-Okayama, 62
San Jose Police Department, 42, 43
San Jose Progress Committee, 25
San Jose Rotary Club, 88
SAn Jose School District, 68
San Jose State, 29, 59
San Jose State College, 33, 43, 57, 59, 61, 68, 74, 76, 80, 81, 82, 83, 85, 90,
92, 93, 96
San Jose State Football Team, 84
San Jose State Teachers College, 14, 93
San Jose State University, 15, 21, 28, 34, 49, 94
San Jose Trolley Corporation, 99, 101
San Jose Unified School District, 75, 76, 88
San Jose USO, 32
San Jose Water Works, 73
San Jose Young Women's Christian Association, 20
San Jose's Latin American Library, 27

San Jose's USO Hut, 31
San Juan Hill, 58
San Leandro, 96
San Salvador Street, 53
Sand Island, 84
Santa Clara, 8, 54, 59
Santa Clara County, 3, 4, 9, 10, 11, 13, 16, 34, 35, 44, 47, 70, 77, 87, 89
Santa Clara County Association for Good Government, 43
Santa Clara County Council on Aging, 68
Santa Clara County Courthouse, 5
Santa Clara County Flood Control & Water Conservation District, 5
Santa Clara County Hospital, 70
Santa Clara County Science School, Boulder Creek, 15
Santa Clara County's Sixth District PTA Braille Transcription Project, 44
Santa Clara Street, 4, 12, 24
Santa Clara Valley, 3, 7, 9, 16, 21, 27, 53, 60, 66, 90
Santa Clara Valley Blind Center, 44
Santa Clara Valley Council for Civic Unity, 13
Santa Clara Valley Water Conservation District, 4, 5, 82
Santa Clara Valley Water District, 89
Santa Cruz, 14
Santa Cruz Mountains, 21, 36, 37
Santa Lucia Range, 21
Saratoga, 8, 49, 61
Sato, Kenzo, 62
Seattle, 97
Second & Santa Clara Streets, 77
Sellers, Benjamin (Honest Ben), 78
Sellers, Margaret Delores, 78
Sepulveda, Nora, 27
Seventh Street, 14
Shasta Avenue, 45
Shawnee, Oklahoma, 20
Shortridge, Charles, 102
Shortridge, Samuel, M., 102
Sierra Nevada Mountains, 9, 39
Silva, Dorothy, 64
Slavit, Norma, 8
Smith, Olney, 59
Smith, Ruth, 59
South Bay Aqueduct, 5
South Eighth Street, 73
South Fifth Street, 24, 51, 61
South San Jose, 64
Southern Pacific Railroad, 33, 58
Spartan, 83, 84, 85
Spartan Daily, 80, 85
Spencer, Francis, 102
Squatrito, Sebastian "Scrappy", 85
St. Albert the Great Church in Palo Alto, 78
St. James Park, 53
St. Joseph's Grammar School, 77
Stanford, 15
Stanford University, 24, 68, 82
Stanford Law School, 4
Stanford Medical School, 70
Stanger, Ken, 84
Starbird, George, 75
State Department of Rehabilitation, 71
Stephens, C.C., 103
Stevens Creek, 4
Stevens Creek Park, 9
Stockton, 47, 93, 99
Stockton Avenue, 100
Sullivan, George L., 59
Sunnyvale, 36
Sunsweet Growers, 10, 66
Sussex, England, 21
Sweeney, Ben, 14, 15
Sweeney, Charles & Ida, 14, 15
Sweeney, Donald, 15
Sweeney, Mardell, 14
Sweeney, Dr. William G. "Bill", 14, 15
Tacoma, Washington, 7
Tainan, Taiwan, 61
Technology Center of Silicon Valley, 52
Temple Emanu-El, 31
The Bell, 86, 87
The Leader, 79

The Villages, 87
Third Street, 53
Thirteenth & Julian Streets, 78
Thompson, State Senator Jack, 5
Topaz, Utah, 98
Topeka, Kansas, 74
Torres, Rita, 27, 29
Trevor-Roper, H. R., 61
True Life Church, 64
Truman, President Harry, 79
Twelfth Street, 17
Twenty-First Street, 12
United Farm Workers Union, 34
United New Conservationists, 89
United Service Organizations, 30
United States Army, 56
United States Mint, 79
United States Navy Medical Corps, 82
United Way, 32
University of Alberta Canada, 98
University of California, Berkeley, 68
University of California, San Diego, 96
University of California, School of Veterinary Medicine, Davis, 10
University of California's Hastings College of Law, 76
University of Hawaii, 84
Univeristy of Illinois, 82
University of Michigan, 74
University of Oregon, 95
University of Santa Clara, 53, 57, 77, 78
University of Santa Clara School of Engineering, 59
University of Toledo, 74
University of Washington, 95
USO Hut, 31
Vallejo, 56

Valley Fair, 53
Valley Medical Center, 39, 70, 72
Van Buren, President Martin, 74
Vasona Dam, 4, 6
Veracruz, Mexico, 61
Villa, Francisco, "Pancho", 49
Viola Avenue, 51
Visiting Nurses Association, 68
Waikiki, 84, 85
Warren, Earl, 79
Washington School, 28
Washington Square, 93
Water Conservation District, 6
Watson, Bernard John "Barney", 88
Watson, Fred, 25, 47, 75
Weber, Angela M., 7
West Alma Street, 50
West Point, 88
White Death, 70
White Scourge, 70
William Street, 61
Willow Glen, 14, 33, 52, 53, 54, 58
Willow Street, 14, 27
Winchester, Sarah, 36
Winchester Mystery House, 66
Winkelman, Coach Ben, 84
Wisconsin, 65
Woodrow Wilson Junior High School, 28
World War I, 50, 59, 99
World War II, 16, 19, 24, 49, 56, 57, 61, 79, 82
Wunder, Jean L., 21
Yasui, Minoru, 95, 96, 97, 98
YMCA, 43
Yuba City, 34
YWCA, 43

109